NARRATIVES

in
Popular Culture,
Media,
and
Everyday Life

NARRATIVES

in
Popular Culture,
Media,
and
Everyday Life

Arthur Asa Berger

SAGE Publications
International Educational and Professional Publisher
Thousand Oaks London New Delhi

In Chapter 2, some material appears from *Morphology of the Folktale*, Second Edition, by Vladimir Propp, translated by Laurence Scott, Revised and Edited with a Preface by Louis A. Wagner, Copyright © 1968. By permission of the University of Texas Press.

For information address:

SAGE Publications, Inc.
2455 Teller Road
Thousand Oaks, California 91320
E-mail: order@sagepub.com

SAGE Publications Ltd.
6 Bonhill Street
London EC2A 4PU
United Kingdom

SAGE Publications India Pvt. Ltd.
M-32 Market
Greater Kailash I
New Delhi 110 048 India

Printed in the United States of America

Library of Congress Cataloging-in-Publication Data

Berger, Arthur Asa, 1933-
  Narratives in popular culture, media, and everyday life / Arthur Asa Berger.
    p. cm.
  Includes bibliographical references (p.) and index.
  ISBN 0-7619-0344-5 (cloth : acid-free paper). — ISBN 0-7619-0345-3 (pbk. : acid-free paper)
    1. Discourse analysis, Narrative. 2. Narration (Rhetoric) 3. Mass media and language. I. Title.
  P302.7.B43 1996
  401'.41—dc20   96-25182

This book is printed on acid-free paper.

97 98 99 00 01 10 9 8 7 6 5 4 3 2

Acquiring Editor: Margaret Seawell
Editorial Assistant: Reneé Piernot
Production Editor: Astrid Virding
Production Assistant: Karen Wiley
Typesetter/Designer: Danielle Dillahunt
Cover Designer: Candace Harman

Contents

Preface

When I was in the middle of writing this book I had an epiphany, a sudden "illumination." Although I had never thought about it before, I realized that I've been writing about narratives for more than 30 years, without being aware of doing so. In fact, much—if not most—of what I've written in my career as a professor and a writer has been about narratives of one kind or another.

What? Me a Narratologist?

The narrative aspects of the topics I've investigated—comics, television shows, popular culture genres, jokes, and so on—always were somewhat hidden, even though I often mentioned narratives from time to time. My first book, *Li'l Abner: A Study in American Satire,* contains a chapter on the narrative elements in the strip, and in it I suggest the usefulness of considering narrativity in dealing with comic strips and comic books.

Although I have written about narratives in my books, it never before occurred to me that a kind of vague, subliminal, unconscious, and unrecognized interest in narratives pervades my work. I started writing this book because I kept coming across references to narratives in many of the books I read, and I became interested in the subject. I had also written a book on genres, so there was a logic to my turning my attention to narratives. My book on genres, one could say, looks at narratives in terms of genre; this book, reversing matters, looks at genres in terms of their narrative dimensions.

Narratives as a "Hot" Subject

Narratives, for one reason or another, have recently become a topic of considerable interest in contemporary literary and cultural studies. Narratives provide a powerful way of teaching people lessons and transmitting ideas. Furthermore, our attitudes toward narratives, some commentators claim, have played a role in shaping contemporary American culture and society. For example, Jean-François Lyotard's *The Postmodern Condition* (1984) includes numerous discussions of narratives (not always fictional ones), and Lyotard even suggests that narratives are at the heart of postmodernism. He writes, "Simplifying to the extreme, I define *postmodernism* as incredulity toward metanarratives" (p. xxiv). By this he means that the grand social and political theories that have organized our lives (which he calls metanarratives) are no longer dominant, and this leads to all kinds of interesting and chaotic results—one of which is our postmodern society.

The Design of This Book

The first part of this book is devoted to a number of theoretical questions: How are narratives defined? How do narratives function? What are the basic components of narratives? What are the basic techniques and devices found in narratives? How does one make sense of narratives? I've tried to take some rather complex ideas—many aspects of narrative theory are quite deep, and at times almost unfathomable— and make them understandable.

In Chapters 5 through 12, I use a rather simple human development model as the organizing structure. I trace narratives from our earliest experience with them, which I suggest is in our dreams, to narratives that play important roles in our adolescent and adult lives. I also address narrative aspects of everyday life, such as jokes, conversations, therapy, and habits (what I call *repeat performances*). Finally, I suggest a project for studying people's lives—that is, personal narratives. The appendix that concludes the volume contains some suggested creative and analytic projects relating to narratives that involve applying what has been discussed in the preceding chapters.

What This Book Will Do for You

It is my hope that this book will help you to understand and interpret a number of different kinds of narratives and to recognize the impacts these narratives may have on your life. Thus I discuss here, and ask you to consider, your dreams, the fairy tales you were exposed to as a young child, the programs you watch on television, the films you see, the comic strips and books and novels you read, the popular culture in which your life is immersed (and that shapes it?), the jokes you tell, and even a number of the things you do from day to day.

This book is about narratives, but really it is about you, the reader. The subtext concerns how narratives shape our perceptions of ourselves and others and how they have affected and continue to have impacts upon our lives, our culture, and society in general. Perhaps as you read this book you will have an epiphany or two of your own, and recognize the roles that narratives have played in your life. If that happens, the time and effort I've spent in writing this book will have been worthwhile.

Acknowledgments

I would like to express my appreciation to my editor, Alex Schwartz, for his support. I also want to thank my production editor, Astrid Virding, and my copy editor, Judy Selhorst, for their assistance with this book. This is my eighth book for Sage Publications, and I have had a long and happy relationship with the editors, production staff, and marketing staff there. I've even convinced my editors, in recent years, to print more of my drawings to give my books a bit more visual interest.

I also owe a debt of gratitude to the following for permission to reprint material here: to the University of Texas Press for the use of material from Vladimir Propp's *Morphology of the Folktale* in Chapter 2; to Universal Press Syndicate for the use of the text from an episode of *Calvin and Hobbes,* by Bill Watterson, in Chapter 7 and to King Features for permission to reprint an episode of *The Katzenjammer Kids;* to Apple Computer, Inc., for the use of the storyboard of the company's famous "1984" television commercial in Chapter 8; and to Stan Freberg for the use of a classic radio commercial script in Chapter 10.

From morning to night, narrations constantly haunt streets and buildings. They articulate our existences by teaching us what they must be. They "cover the event," that is to say, they *make* our legends (*legenda*, what is to be read and said) out of it. Captured by the radio (the voice is the law) as soon as he awakens, the listener walks all day long through the forest of narrativities from journalism, advertising, and television narrativities that still find time, as he is getting ready for bed, to slip a few final messages under the portals of sleep. Even more than the God told about by the theologians of earlier days, these stories have a providential and predestining function: they organize in advance our work, our celebrations, and even our dreams. Social life multiplies the gestures and modes of behavior *(im)printed* by narrative models; it . . . reproduces and accumulates "copies" of stories. Our society has become a recited society, in three senses: it is defined by *stories* (*recits*, the fables constituted by our advertising and informational media), by *citations* of stories, and by the interminable *recitation* of stories.

Michel de Certeau, *The Practice of Everyday Life* (1984, p. 186)

1

The Nature of Narratives

We seldom think about it, but we spend our lives immersed in narratives. Every day, we swim in a sea of stories and tales that we hear or read or listen to or see (or some combination of all of these), from our earliest days to our deaths. And our deaths are recorded in narratives, also—for that's what obituaries are. As Peter Brooks (1984) puts it: "Our lives are ceaselessly intertwined with narrative, with the stories that we tell, all of which are reworked in that story of our own lives that we narrate to ourselves. . . . We are immersed in narrative" (p. 3).

In this book I will discuss a number of topics related to narratives. What are narratives? How do they differ from other kinds of literary works? Why are they important to us? What roles do narratives have in our lives? How do narratives function?

I should note that I adopt here the term used in literary theory to refer to creative works of all kinds, *text*. This enables me to talk about everything from comic strips to novels without having to repeat myself all the time and signifies that what is being discussed, the text, is some kind of a work of art—low or high, popular or elite, for children or adults. *Text* is an abstract and general term that can be very useful, especially when one is dealing with theoretical matters.

We are exposed to narrative texts from our earliest days, when our mothers sing lullabies and recite nursery rhymes for us. The songs and simple verse we learn when we are small children are narratives. For example, take the nursery rhyme about Humpty Dumpty:

> *Humpty Dumpty sat on a wall,*
> *Humpty Dumpty had a great fall;*
> *All the king's horses*
> *And all the king's men*
> *Couldn't put Humpty Dumpty together again.*

This is a narrative text—a simple one, but a narrative nevertheless. So are fairy tales, adventure stories, biographies, detective stories, and science fiction stories. Television is a narrative medium par excellence. It is possible to see the evening news shows on television as narratives (or as having many narrative elements in them), although the people who create newscasts would probably find that idea somewhat far-fetched. Comic strips are narratives, but single-frame cartoons are not. Such cartoons give us a moment in time, but they contain no sequence, generally speaking.

Although narratives may be simple or complex, understanding how they function and how people make sense of them are subjects that are extremely complicated and that have perplexed literary theorists for centuries—from at least as far back as Aristotle's time to the present.

Speculations About Humpty Dumpty

Let's consider the information the little nursery rhyme about Humpty Dumpty gives us.

1. Humpty Dumpty. Humpty Dumpty is the name of a character, the hero, whose "tragic fate" is the subject of the story. We also have an example of personification, as an egg is turned into a person (although the rhyme does not specify that Humpty Dumpty is an egg, this element of the story is understood through tradition and reinforced by illustrations that have accompanied the rhyme in countless publications). There is also an internal rhyme in the name (the repetition of "umpty") that adds emphasis.

Interestingly, a case can be made that Humpty Dumpty isn't just a nonsense name. The word *hump* refers to a rounded protuberance of some kind, and *dump* can refer to the emptying out of a container (as in dump truck); thus "Humpty Dumpty" is a rounded protuberance that empties itself out—which is precisely what happens in the story. Of course, both *hump* and *dump* have other meanings as well, but without stretching things too much we can see a relationship between Humpty Dumpty's name and what happens to him.

2. *Sat.* Here an action or, perhaps more accurately, an activity is described. Humpty Dumpty is doing something—in this case sitting on a wall. Something is about to happen, so we can say that we have "rising action" here—though we know it will soon be falling action.

3. *On a wall.* Here we have location and spatiality. Where is Humpty Dumpty sitting? On a wall—though we don't know where the wall is. Walls generally have some height, so we have reason to believe (and we know from traditional illustrations of the rhyme) that he is quite a distance from the ground.

4. *Humpty Dumpty.* Once again the name of the main character appears. Such repetition is a way of generating emphasis.

5. *Had a great fall.* With this description of more action, Humpty Dumpty's crisis is related. This is the crucial event in this simple story. The word *fall* can be connected to many different kinds of events, from the fall of Adam and Eve to other kinds of falling, sometimes good (falling in love) and sometimes not so good (falling into debt, falling behind in payments).

6. *All the king's horses.* This part of the rhyme is puzzling. What do the king's horses have to do with anything? The line suggests, implicitly, the power of the king and the nature of the king's commitment. He committed all his horses to a task. The horses actually are secondary characters in this story, as we shall see.

7. And all the king's men. This line adds emphasis to the one preceding it through repetition, and together these two lines suggest that even if the king committed all his resources to the matter of putting Humpty Dumpty together again, it still could not be done. There are limitations, then, on what kings can do and, by implication, limitations on what anyone can do in given situations. The king's men and, by inference, the king are actually secondary characters in this tale. The two lines "All the king's horses / And all the king's men" represent a response to Humpty Dumpty's fall and can be thought of as part of "falling action." The main event has occurred, other secondary things are going on, but in a sense the story has had its crisis.

8. Couldn't put Humpty Dumpty together again. With this line we reach the "tragic" resolution of the story. Nobody—not even the king, with all his horses and all his men—could put Humpty Dumpty together again— nobody can reconstruct an egg that has fallen and splattered.

We can see that even a simple nursery rhyme has the basic components of a narrative, even if they are elemental in nature. Such narratives are well suited for the intellectual capacities and emotional development of their target audience—young children. As we get older and grow more mature, we become interested in narrative texts that are more challenging and more complicated. These texts require more of us; we need more refined sensibilities and more information, as well, to understand and appreciate them.

What Is a Narrative?

A narrative is, as I have suggested, a story, and stories tell about things that have happened or are happening to people, animals, aliens from outer space, insects—whatever. That is, a story contains a sequence of events, which means that narratives take place within or over, to be more precise, some kind of time period. This time period can be very short, as in a nursery tale, or very long, as in some novels and epics. Many stories are linear in structure, which may be represented as follows:

$$A \rightarrow B \rightarrow C \rightarrow D \rightarrow E \rightarrow F \rightarrow G \rightarrow H \rightarrow I$$

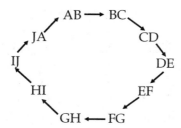

Figure 1.1. The Circular Nature of *La Ronde*

In this case, A leads to B, which leads to C, and so on, until the story ends with I.

Stories need not always follow straight lines, however; they can also move in circles or in other configurations. Consider the play *La Ronde* (The Circle), which can be diagrammed as follows:

AB → BC → CD → DE → EF → FG → GH → HI → IJ → JA

However, a diagram of *La Ronde* that shows its circular nature, such as that in Figure 1.1, gives a better idea of what happens in the play. *La Ronde* has a plot in which the motion is circular: A has a relationship with B, B has a relationship with C, and so on until J has a relationship with A and the circle is, so to speak, closed.

The 10 "dialogues" or scenes of *La Ronde* are described by Arthur Schnitzler (1897), the author of the play, as follows:

1. AB: the Whore and the Soldier
2. BC: the Soldier and the Parlour Maid
3. CD: the Parlour Maid and the Young Gentleman
4. DE: the Young Gentleman and the Young Wife
5. EF: the Young Wife and the Husband
6. FG: the Husband and the Little Miss
7. GH: the Little Miss and the Poet
8. HI: the Poet and the Actress
9. IJ: the Actress and the Count
10. JA: the Count and the Whore

Thus the circle is complete when the Count and the Whore have their dialogue.

Although Schnitzler calls his scenes "dialogues," various actions also take place in each scene, so that term is not quite accurate. There are, of course, plays in which almost no action is shown—in which actors (functioning as narrators of sorts) read letters between characters and that sort of thing—but most of the time plays depict actions; that is, characters do other things as well as talk. Talking, of course, can also be construed as a kind of action.

Notice that I used the term *plot* above regarding *La Ronde*. Is there a difference between a plot and a story? If so, how does a plot relate to a story? I will discuss this matter later, but I mention it here to show that there are complications that we must deal with when discussing narratives.

The Differences Between
Narratives and Nonnarratives

As I have stated, narratives, in the most simple sense, are stories that take place in time. What else might we say about them? One topic we should deal with involves the way narratives differ from nonnarratives. Consider, for example, the story about Humpty Dumpty and a drawing of Humpty Dumpty shown sitting on a wall. In the story we find out what happened to Humpty Dumpty—he had a fall and couldn't be put back together again. (This simple story, I might add, is used endlessly by writers and speakers to make points about the frailty of institutions and about the nature of life; sometimes, Humpty Dumpty serves to teach us, we tear things apart and find that we can't put them back together again. So we learn something from this tale.) In the picture, we see Humpty Dumpty sitting on the wall and that is all. We capture a moment in time, but we do not see any sequence.

Drawings, paintings, photographs—anything pictorial, in one frame—are not generally thought to be narratives, though they may be parts of narratives that we all know and are familiar with. For example, comic strips are made up of frames; each frame captures a moment in time, and the collection of frames takes place in time. Drawings of Humpty Dumpty are part of the common knowledge of young children in England and the United States (and perhaps elsewhere); when they see a picture of Humpty Dumpty sitting on the wall, they know what will happen because they've been exposed to the nursery rhyme as part of their childhood culture.

Although some paintings contain enough information that they can be read as narratives, with the viewer looking at one part of the painting and then moving on to another, generally speaking, pictures that stand alone are not understood to have narrative content.

Narration and Narratives

A narrator is someone who tells a story. The word comes from the Latin *narratus*, which means "made known." A narrator makes something—a story—known, whether one created by another or by the narrator him- or herself, as in the case of a storyteller. Take the nursery rhyme we've been discussing, "Humpty Dumpty." Technically speaking, this story is narrated.

Humpty Dumpty is an object, but not a subject. That is, he is someone whose tragic fate is described by a narrator, but Humpty Dumpty says nothing and does not relate to others. We can make a distinction, then, between *subjects*, who act and relate to others, and *objects*, whose actions are described by narrators. Sometimes, of course, narrators tell about others—objects—but also assume roles of characters who are described and may even contribute dialogue, but this dialogue always is related by the narrators.

But not all stories are related by narrators or have narrators in them. Some stories, as we have seen, have narrators who more or less introduce the stories and are found in them from time to time, explaining things or introducing new aspects of the stories, but other stories have no narrators. These stories are simply "acted out" by the characters, so to speak, one of whom generally functions as a narrator but isn't a narrator per se. We watch what the characters do, listen to what they say, and get a sense of the story—without the need for a narrator. Consider this nursery rhyme:

> *Baa, baa, black sheep,*
> *Have you any wool?*
> *Yes, sir, yes, sir,*

Three bags full:
One for my master,
And one for my dame,
And one for the little boy
Who lives down the lane.

In this very elemental narrative we have dialogue between a male person ("sir") and a black sheep, and the dialogue tells the story. The "sir" figure asks a question and the black sheep answers. It is a simple story, of course, but it is a story nevertheless. There is sequence here and a story to be told. We also learn, incidentally, that the black sheep has a master and a dame and knows a little boy who lives down the lane. Giving information to the reader, as we shall see later in this volume, is often an important part of narratives. Narratives don't always have to include physical action.

In some stories the narrator is present, whereas in others the narrator is more or less "hidden." Fairy tales, for example, which traditionally start out, "Once upon a time," have narrators. These narrators often introduce the characters and then disappear (though not always), but they are there at the beginning.

We can say, then, that in many narrated stories, it is the narrator who tells the story about certain characters. In other stories, the narrator introduces the story and then recedes into the background. There are combinations of these styles as well; sometimes a narrator tells a story, but we also find characters talking with one another and interacting so as to carry the story.

In Lewis Carroll's *Through the Looking Glass* (1872/1960), we come upon Humpty Dumpty again, but in this rendering of the story we have Alice talking with Humpty Dumpty:

> "It's *very* provoking," Humpty Dumpty said after a long silence, looking away from Alice as he spoke, "to be called an egg—*very!*"
> "I said you *looked* like an egg, Sir," Alice gently explained. "And some eggs are very pretty, you know," she added, hoping to turn her remark into a sort of compliment. (p. 181)

This dialogue between Humpty Dumpty and Alice goes on at considerable length, and includes the famous business about un-birthdays and so on. What Carroll has done here is dramatize the traditional nursery rhyme by turning Humpty Dumpty into a subject, a character who interacts with another character, Alice.

I should point out that in stories, as Yuri Lotman (1977) has suggested, everything has significance. As Lotman notes, "The tendency to interpret *everything* in an artistic text as meaningful is so great that we rightfully consider nothing accidental in a work of art" (p. 17). Of course, some things are more significant than others. In some cases, *lack* of certain kinds of action must be construed as action. For example, in a famous Sherlock Holmes story, a dog that doesn't bark (because it recognizes its master) is the key to solving the mystery. In stories, then, we can say that everything plays a role and nothing is completely irrelevant, even though it may seem to be at first sight. That is one of the keys to detective stories: Things that seem inconsequential are later shown, when the detective solves the crime, to be significant.

Why Narratives Are Important

As I mentioned earlier, narratives pervade our lives. When we are young children, our mothers and fathers (and others) sing us lullabies and other songs and teach us to recite nursery rhymes, and as we get older we are read fairy tales and other stories, and eventually we learn to read stories ourselves. These stories play important roles in our lives. For instance, Bruno Bettelheim (1976) has suggested that fairy tales actually help children to deal with psychological issues. He asserts that fairy tales can generate messages to an individual's conscious, preconscious, and unconscious mind—depending upon which level the person is functioning on at a given time. Fairy tales deal with problems that are universal, issues that tend to preoccupy a child's mind. They have meaning for the child's ego and encourage its development; at the same time, they relieve preconscious and unconscious pressures the child may be experiencing. In addition, they acknowledge id pressures a child may feel and show the child ways to satisfy these pressures that are acceptable to his or her ego and superego.

Bettelheim uses Freud's typology (his "structural hypothesis"), in which he suggests that the human psyche has three components: the id, which roughly approximates drives and impulses; the superego, which can be equated with guilt, conscience, and moral sensibilities; and the ego, which tries to mediate between the id and superego and which concerns itself with monitoring the world and surviving.

What Bettelheim says, among other things, is that we learn from fairy tales; we can extend his argument and say that we learn from narratives. In fact, some scholars suggest that one of the most important ways we learn about the world, and ourselves as well, is through narratives. As Laurel Richardson (1990) writes:

> Narrative is the primary way through which humans organize their experiences into temporally meaningful episodes. . . .
> Narrative is both a mode of reasoning *and* a mode of representation. People can "apprehend" the world narratively and people can "tell" about the world narratively. According to Jerome Bruner (1986) narrative reasoning is one of the two basic and universal human cognition modes. The other mode is the logico-scientific. . . . the logico-scientific mode looks for universal truth conditions, whereas the narrative mode looks for particular connections between events. Explanation in the narrative mode is contextually embedded, whereas the logico-scientific explanation is extracted from spatial and temporal events. Both modes are "rational" ways of making meaning. (p. 118)

Clearly, narratives are very important to us; they furnish us with both a method for learning about the world and a way to tell others what we have learned. Narrative is not external to the logico-scientific mode; scientists must use narratives in recounting their experiments, and experiments, which have both linear and sequential dimensions, can be seen as having a narrative structure.

Another way we learn about things is through figurative language—through metaphor, which is based on analogy, and through metonymy, which is based on association. These two modes are compared in Table 1.1. The last items in the table are examples of subcategories of each: simile, a weaker form of metaphor that uses *like* or *as*, and synecdoche, a form of metonymy in which part stands for the whole or vice versa. Sometimes an object can be employed as both metaphor and metonym. A snake, for example, metaphorically brings to mind (i.e., vaguely resembles, by being long and thin) a penis and also is

TABLE 1.1 Metaphor and Metonymy

Metaphor	*Metonymy*
analogy	association
My love is a red rose.	Rolls Royce = wealth
My love is like a rose.	Pentagon = American military
(simile)	(synecdoche)

associated with Eve and the Garden of Eden, and thus has metonymic significance.

We tend to think of metaphor and metonymy as literary devices that are far removed from our everyday lives, but this is not the case. As George Lakoff and Mark Johnson (1980) note:

> Metaphor is pervasive in everyday life, not just in language but in thought and action. Our ordinary conceptual system, in terms of which we both think and act, is fundamentally metaphoric in nature. The concepts that govern our thought are not just matters of the intellect. They also govern our everyday functioning, down to the most mundane details. Our concepts structure what we perceive, how we get around in the world, and how we relate to other people. Our conceptual system thus plays a central role in defining our everyday realities. If we are right in suggesting that our conceptual system is largely metaphorical, then the way we think, what we experience, and what we do every day is very much a matter of metaphor. (p. 3)

We must remember, of course, that metaphors and metonyms are found in all kinds of narratives. Humpty Dumpty, remember, is an egg, and thus there is metaphoric significance to this little nursery rhyme—which is one of the reasons the story is so resonant.

We can make a distinction between conceptual knowledge, which is theoretical and involves abstract ideas (metaphorical in nature, if Lakoff & Johnson are correct), and actualized conceptions, which involve putting concepts into narratives and teaching by "exemplification." One can say, using abstract ideas, "Certain phenomena or entities when disassembled can never be assembled again to represent their former state." The Humpty Dumpty story exemplifies this in a most memorable way.

Reading Narratives   ,

Narratives rely on their readers' having stores of information that make it possible for them to understand what is going on. If a reader does not know what a sheep is, what wool is, what a master is, and what a dame is, "Baa, Baa, Black Sheep" doesn't make any sense. Stories aimed at young children tend to deal with animals and other figures they have learned about and have relatively simple plots. As children develop and their stores of information increase, the stories they read demand more of them. Writers of stories aimed at adults usually assume that we will understand or be able to make sense of everything they write.

The Role of the Reader

Reader-response theorists, or reception theorists, point out that texts require readers to fill in a lot of blank areas and suggest that different readers fill in these blanks in different ways. That is why no two people read a given text the same way—though there may be a great deal of similarity between what one person gets out of reading *The Maltese Falcon,* for example, and what another person gets out of it. As Donald McCloskey (1990) notes:

> The fictional writer selects like the scientist, and invites the reader to fill in the blanks. Stories or articles can give only a sample of experience, because experience is overwhelmed by irrelevance: taking out the rubbish, bumping the table, scratching the back of one's head, seeing the title of the book one was not looking for. What distinguishes the good storyteller and the good scientific thinker from the bad is a sense of pointedness. (p. 19)

That is, no work of fiction can tell everything. Writers select certain things to tell and assume that readers will enrich what they read with their own fund of knowledge.

McCloskey quotes from Wolfgang Iser, one of the leading spokesmen for reception theory:

> What is missing from the apparently trivial scenes, the gaps arising out of the dialogue—this is what stimulates the reader into filling the blanks

TABLE 1.2 Relations Between Texts and Reader

Texts	*(Work)*	*Reader*
author		reader, audience
artistic plane		aesthetic plane
sender		receiver
creates a text		realizes a text
text as a system of signs to be understood		text as a site for creation of meaning

SOURCE: Berger (1995a).

> with projections [the image is of the reader running a motion picture inside his head, which is of course why novels can still compete with television]. . . . the "enduring form of life" which Virginia Woolf speaks of is not manifested on the printed page; it is a product arising out of the interaction between text and reader. (p. 19)

The image we get from Iser is one of texts as full of holes, with readers of the texts filling in these holes, in the same manner that readers of comic strips and comic books, for example, fill in the continuity between the frames.

Iser (1972/1988) makes a distinction between two poles, what he calls the "artistic" and the "aesthetic." He explains this notion as follows:

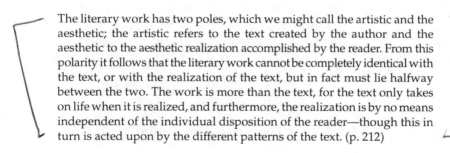

> The literary work has two poles, which we might call the artistic and the aesthetic; the artistic refers to the text created by the author and the aesthetic to the aesthetic realization accomplished by the reader. From this polarity it follows that the literary work cannot be completely identical with the text, or with the realization of the text, but in fact must lie halfway between the two. The work is more than the text, for the text only takes on life when it is realized, and furthermore, the realization is by no means independent of the individual disposition of the reader—though this in turn is acted upon by the different patterns of the text. (p. 212)

Berkeley, the philosopher, has said, "To be is to be perceived." It is, in a sense, the reading of the text, analogous to the act of perception, that brings the text into being, and this creation takes place in highly individualistic ways.

> Every work is rewritten by its reader who imposes upon it a new grid
> of interpretation for which he is not generally responsible but which
> comes to him from his culture, from his time, in short from another
> discourse; all comprehension is the encounter of two discourses, a
> dialogue. It is futile and silly to try to leave off being oneself in order
> to become someone else; were one to succeed, the result would be of
> no interest (since it would be a pure reproduction of the initial
> discourse). By its very existence, the science of ethnology proves to us,
> if need be, that we *gain* by being different from what we seek to
> understand. This interpretation (in the necessary double sense of
> translation and comprehension) is the condition of survival of the
> antecedent text; but no less so, I should say, of contemporary
> discourse. Hence interpretation is no longer true or false but rich or
> poor, revealing or sterile, stimulating or dull.
>
> Tzvetan Todorov, *Introduction to Poetics* (1981, p. xxx)

Table 1.2 provides a clearer picture of Iser's ideas. From this perspective, the readers of texts (and by *readers* I mean people who watch
television, see films, play video games, and so on) play a much more
important role than they are perceived to play in other theories.

There are some problems with reader-response theories that connect
reader responses to such reader characteristics as social class and gender.
For one thing, people may react viscerally to texts they read or see, and
these reactions may have nothing to do with such things as socioeconomic class and intelligence, but may be more directly connected with
emotion and physical state. In addition, though we may all differ in the
readings we give to texts, the similarities we find in them may be much
more significant than the differences we perceive as a result of differing
educational levels, cultural codings, and so on.

The Place of Narratives in the Media

Let me offer a model that places narratives and all kinds of texts into
a context, so we can see where texts fit in the larger scheme of things.
Texts are created by individuals (or groups of people in collaborative
media, such as film and television) and are written for audiences of one
sort or another. They are communicated to others via some medium: the

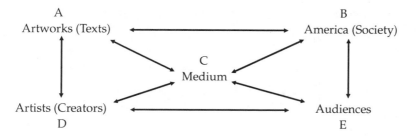

Figure 1.2. Focal Points in Analysis of Media

spoken word, radio, print, television, film, the Internet—whatever. All of this takes place in a particular society. (Many works, however, do become popular in a number of different societies. Some comic strips and novels are translated into a number of languages, and films and television programs often have audiences in many different countries.)

Thus there are five focal points involved in the process of communicating texts (see Figure 1.2). All of these focal points are connected to one another, and we can pay attention to any one of the five elements or deal with various combinations of elements at any given time (for a more detailed discussion of these focal points, see Berger, 1995b).

The texts we are concerned with here are narratives, and our primary focus is upon the way narratives work—how they have an impact on people (audiences) and on society—but we cannot neglect any of the five focal points; we have to think about them in terms of their relations to one another. The medium an artist works in, for example, profoundly affects the texts he or she creates and the way people in audiences respond to the texts. For instance, there is a considerable amount of difference between seeing a film in a theater that has a huge screen and a powerful audio system and seeing that same film on a 19-inch television screen with 3-inch speakers.

One of the things we must do is recognize that many phenomena that we do not think of as narrative texts are, in fact, narratives—or have strong narrative components in them. If conversations, illnesses (which are the subject of many conversations), love affairs, and psychotherapy can be thought of as narratives, that means they have certain characteristics and follow certain rules that we find in more conventional kinds of narratives, or, to be more precise, in texts that we commonly identify and recognize as narratives, such as fairy tales, plays, stories, novels, films, and songs.

Topics to Be Covered in This Book

In this chapter I have suggested what narratives are, how they differ from other kinds of literary and artistic texts, and have discussed the significance narratives have for individuals and for societies. In the chapters that follow I will deal with narrative theory, with artistic devices used in narrative texts, with different kinds of narratives, and with the roles narratives play in our everyday lives.

Let me conclude this chapter by citing an often-heard poem that was used not long ago by a news analyst who was trying to explain why President Clinton seemed to be so unpopular with many American voters (as expressed in the 1994 elections), even though he had been successful in managing the economy and had had a number of foreign relations successes. The analyst was stumped, and to show his inability to locate the source of Clinton's lack of popularity, recited a version of this poem by Thomas Brown, written more than 300 years ago:

> *I do not love thee, Doctor Fell.*
> *The reason why I cannot tell;*
> *But this alone I know full well,*
> *I do not love thee, Doctor Fell.*

In this simple story, a person says he doesn't love Dr. Fell (and tells Dr. Fell so directly), though the speaker cannot offer a good reason for his (or her) feelings. The speaker feels this dislike and that's enough, as far as he (or she) is concerned.

This poem expresses irrational distaste in a brief and compelling manner, and it is often cited by people who are dealing with opinions of others that are not supported by evidence of any kind. As we know, people often vote, buy things, get married, and take other actions on the basis of vague feelings, fugitive passions, and irrational likes and dislikes—such behavior is captured beautifully by this poem.

Numberless are the world's narratives. First of all, in a prodigious variety of genres, themselves distributed among different substances, as if any material were appropriate for man to entrust his stories to it: narrative can be supported by articulated speech, oral or written, by image, fixed or moving, by gesture, and by the organized mixture of all these substances; it is present in myth, legend, fable, tale, tragedy, comedy, epic, history, pantomime, painting (think of Carpaccio's *Saint Ursula*), stained glass window, cinema, comic book, news item, conversation. Further, in these almost infinite forms, narrative occurs in all periods, in all places, all societies; narrative begins with the very history of humanity; there is not, there has never been, any people anywhere without narrative; all classes, all human groups have their narratives, and very often these are enjoyed by men of different, even opposing culture: narrative never prefers good to bad literature: international, transhistorical, transcultural, narrative is *there*, like life.

Roland Barthes, The Semiotic Challenge (1988, p. 89)

2

Theorists of Narrativity

In Chapter 1, I suggested that there is a difference between a narrative and a text that conveys everything all at once (for example, a picture); I said that narratives have sequence, among other things. In this chapter I will discuss the essentials of narratives as elaborated by a few of the more important theorists of the nature of narrativity. The focus is on what narratives have in common, though they all differ in numerous ways. I should note that we will be dealing here, at times, with extremely abstract, technical, and complicated analyses by a number of authors. We begin with the person who was probably the most influential theorist of narrativity, the philosopher Aristotle.

Aristotle on Narratives

In Aristotle's *Poetics*, written about 330 B.C., we find a number of passages that relate to narratives. Aristotle deals with "poetry," but he uses that term in a very general sense to talk about literature in general and narratives in particular, we might say. He starts by suggesting that literary works are imitations of reality (the mimetic theory of art) and notes that we must consider three topics relative to imitation: the medium of imitation, the objects imitated, and the mode of imitation.

He discusses first the media of imitation, mentioning that some arts, prose or verse, use language alone, whereas other arts employ a number of different media. (A modern analogue would be the difference between a novel and a film made from that novel. In the novel, we have only words; in the film, we have actors, dialogue, settings, sound, music, and various other things.) He then addresses the objects of imitation:

> Since the objects of imitation are men in action, and these men must be either of a higher or a lower type (for moral character mainly answers to these divisions, goodness and badness being the distinguishing marks of moral differences), it follows that we must represent men either as better than in real life, or as worse, or as they are. (Aristotle, 1941, in Smith & Parks, 1951, p. 30)

There are, of course, only three possibilities, logically speaking, as Aristotle points out: We can portray people as they are, as better than they are, or as worse than they are. We must keep in mind that we are dealing with "men in action," as he puts it—that is, people doing things, which he later describes as Plot.

This is followed by Aristotle's analysis of his third topic, the manner of imitation. He explains, "The poet may imitate by narration, in which case he can either take another personality, as Homer does, or speak in his own person, unchanged—or he may present all his characters as living and moving before us" (p. 30). What Aristotle does is offer an overview of the nature of literary works and the ways in which they can be structured. There are, he suggests, three possibilities:

1. Assume another's identity (which means one writes in the third person).
2. Speak in your own person (which means one writes in the first person).
3. Have your characters tell the story by interacting with one another.

It is also possible to mix things up. Thus, for example, a novel may begin with a third-person narrator and then move into a situation in which the narrator withdraws and the characters in the story take over.

Aristotle then goes on to differentiate comedy from tragedy. Comedy, he tells us, is "an imitation of persons inferior—not, however, in the full sense of the word bad, the Ludicrous being merely a subdivision of the ugly. It consists of some defect or ugliness which is not painful or destructive" (p. 33). Tragedy, on the other hand, "is an imitation of an action that is serious, complete, and of a certain magnitude" (p. 36).

In his discussion of tragedy, Aristotle analyzes what must be done to present tragedy correctly. He offers a highly schematic discussion of some of the fundamental aspects of narrative:

> Now as tragic imitation implies persons acting, it necessarily follows, in the first place, that Spectacular equipment will be part of Tragedy. Next, Song and Diction, for these are the media of imitation. . . .
>
> Again, Tragedy is the imitation of an action; and an action implies personal agents who necessarily possess certain distinctive qualities both of character and thought; for it is by these that we qualify actions themselves, and these—thought and character—are the two natural causes from which actions spring, and on actions again all success or failure depends. Hence the Plot is the imitation of the action—for by Plot I here mean the arrangement of the incidents. By Character I mean that in virtue of which we ascribe certain qualities to the agents. Thought is required wherever a statement is proved or, it may be, a general truth enunciated. Every Tragedy, therefore, must have six parts, which parts determine its quality—namely Plot, Character, Diction, Thought, Spectacle, Melody. Two of the parts constitute the medium of imitation, one the manner, and three the objects of imitation. And these complete the list. (p. 34)

Here Aristotle mentions a number of the more important aspects of narrative theory as it relates to texts—plot, characters, and dialogue (which is more or less what he means by "Diction")—but most important of all, he insists, is the "the structure of the incidents," or plot. What the characters do, he reminds us, is connected to what they are like and how they think. Readers of novels, for instance, must find out at certain times (through various techniques used by authors) what the characters think as well as follow what they do.

Aristotle also asserts that tragedy involves an imitation of action that is whole, complete, and unified, suggesting that if any one of the components of a work is displaced, the work will be "disjointed and disturbed." In addition, the poet deals not only with what has happened but also with what may happen—with, as Aristotle puts it, "what is possible according to the law of probability or necessity" (p. 37). Because works should have unity, Aristotle does not like episodic plots, those in which "episodes or acts succeed one another without probable or necessary sequence" (p. 38).

Aristotle distinguishes between simple plots and complex plots. Simple plots involve changes of fortune without reversals or recognition by the major characters as to what has happened. Complex plots involve changes of fortune with reversals or recognitions, or both. By "recognition," Aristotle means "a change from ignorance to knowledge, producing love or hate between the persons destined by the poet for good or bad fortune" (p. 39). The best plots have both reversals and recognition and involve changes of fortune from good to bad that arouse both fear and pity.

This has been only a brief summary of a number of the most important points Aristotle makes in his *Poetics* concerning the nature of narratives. He discusses many of the topics I have mentioned in considerably more detail, of course, and a number of other topics that I have not addressed, but the preceding discussion, I believe, conveys a reasonable idea of Aristotle's theories on narrativity. We must remember that Aristotle's philosophy carried tremendous weight, and his ideas have influenced the thinking of writers and critics for thousands of years and are still influential to this day, though they don't have the authority they did in earlier times.

Of course, like the works of all great thinkers, Aristotle's writings have been interpreted and reinterpreted over the ages, and people have debated what Aristotle "really" meant. Still, his theory that art imitates reality is one of the dominant theories of how art functions. Art is, he argues, a *mirror*, reflecting reality. (The other dominant theories of art are that art is like a *lamp*, projecting its own reality rather than imitating reality; that art is a *tool* with essentially pragmatic functions, such as to teach or to indoctrinate; and that art is a *record* and essentially expresses the emotions and feelings and state of mind of the artist. These theories are discussed in some detail in M. H. Abrams's book *The Mirror and The Lamp*, 1958.)

We now move to a discussion of the work of a more contemporary theorist, Vladimir Propp, whose study of folktales has been extremely influential and useful to narrative theorists.

Vladimir Propp on the Problems
of Studying Folktales

Vladimir Propp first published his classic study *Morphology of the Folktale* in 1928, but an English edition of the book did not appear until 30 years later. It is generally acknowledged to be one of the most important studies of the nature of narratives, even though it focuses on a particular group of Russian fairy tales. The term *morphology* refers to the study of structures or forms, looking at the components of some system and seeing how they relate to one another. In botany, *morphology* refers to the study of the component parts of a plant, of their relationship to each other and to the whole—in other words, the study of the plant's structure.

Propp's morphology is not of plants but of folktales. He indicates that he has taken this approach because he believes that other approaches to folktales have been inadequate. He chastises some folklorists who argue that they cannot collect sufficient amounts of material to analyze certain folktales because there are so many variants of the stories in existence. Propp suggests that the various classification schemes folklorists have developed to classify folktales into discrete categories are unworkable. The same applies to attempts to classify folktales according to their themes and other systems that try to make sense of folktales on the basis of types, categories, or motifs. He mentions, for example, the work of Veselovskij, who claims to have found certain motifs, the most basic units of narratives, that are allegedly indivisible; Propp shows that these motifs often can indeed be divided.

Propp concludes, then, that attempts to study folktales in terms of their historical origins or themes or types of characters lead nowhere. He asserts that what is needed is a means of making a morphological analysis of folktales. Such analysis can make historical studies and intelligent comparisons of texts possible. Without some standard way of classifying elements, it is impossible to make intelligent comparisons between and among tales. This is necessary if one wants to address the vexing problem of why so many tales, told in many different parts of the world, are so similar.

Propp argues that there must be a way to separate tales into their components—to develop a morphology of the folktale that will enable readers to isolate the essential components of a tale and see how they relate to each other. Such analysis reveals the structure of narratives—how they are put together.

Morphology of the Folktale

Propp (1928/1968) starts by pointing out that a given action may be done by any number of different characters in a story. This makes it possible to study a story in terms of the functions of its various characters—*functions* being understood as both the actions of characters and the consequences of these actions for the story. According to Propp, the functions of characters are independent of the characters' fulfilling their functions and are the fundamental elements of a story. Propp asserts that there are only a limited number of functions (31), and that the sequence of functions found in folktales and fairy tales is always identical—all such stories have the same structure.

Propp claims that his study of 100 tales gives him more than enough material to derive the functions he names. In the third chapter of *Morphology of the Folktale*, Propp offers a list and description of his functions that includes a conventional sign for each function, an abbreviated definition of each function, and a summary of each function's nature. He then gives a number of examples. All stories begin with what he calls an "initial situation," in which the main characters are introduced; this is not a function. Propp discusses each function in turn; some he deals with in half a page, whereas others require three or four pages to list all of the variations and explain these variations.

As mentioned above, Propp asserts that there are 31 (and no more than 31) functions found in the fairy tales he analyzes, though a given tale might not contain all 31 functions. There are also a number of different subcategories within given functions, so the possible number of combinations of subcategories is immense. Propp's work is of interest to us here because the functions he found in his 100 folktales are not limited to the stories he studied; with minor adaptations, many of his functions can be applied to modern narratives (of all genres) as well.

As Alan Dundes points out in his introduction to the 1968 edition of *Morphology of the Folktale*, Propp's system can be applied to genres other than fairy tales and to other media that carry narratives—novels, plays, comic strips, films, and television programs. We learn from Propp, then, that many modern narratives borrow not content per se, but structure from fairy tales. That is, they use Propp's functions, but in modernized adaptations. Propp's work can help us to understand the "structure" of all kinds of narratives, a subject about which I will have more to say later.

Table 2.1 offers a highly schematic list of Propp's definitions, signs, and functions. The initial situation, as I have noted above, is not considered a function. These are the fundamental components of the 100 tales Propp studied, and they are found also, as Dundes suggests, in many contemporary texts, regardless of medium. Propp has given us a true morphology of narratives: a list of their basic components. We might think of his functions as *narratemes*, which can be defined as the most elemental aspects of stories, the elements out of which narratives of all kinds in all media are constructed.

Of course, in contemporary times, we need to make modifications to some of Propp's functions; for instance, instead of the hero's getting married and ascending the throne, he may get married and get a good job with his father-in-law, or he may not get married but end up making love to the moral (or is it immoral?) equivalent of the princess figure.

TABLE 2.1 Propp's Functions

Function			Description
	α	initial situation	Members of family are introduced; hero is introduced.
1.	β	absentation	One of the members of the family absents him- or herself.
2.	γ	interdiction	Interdiction addressed to hero (can be reversed).
3.	δ	violation	Interdiction is violated.
4.	ε	reconnaissance	Villain makes attempt to get information
5.	ξ	delivery	Villain gets information about victim.
6.	η	trickery	Villain tries to deceive victim.
7.	θ	complicity	Victim is deceived.
8.	A	villainy	Villain causes harm to a member of the family; or
	a	lack	Member of the family lacks something, desires something.
9.	B	mediation	Misfortune made known; hero is dispatched.
10.	C	counteraction	Hero (seeker) agrees to counteraction.
11.	↑	departure	Hero leaves home.
12.	D	1st donor function	Hero tested, receives magical agent or helper.
13.	E	hero's reaction	Hero reacts to agent or donor.
14.	F	receipt of agent	Hero acquires use of magical agent.
15.	G	spatial change	Hero led to object of search.
16.	H	struggle	Hero and villain join in direct combat.
17.	J	branding	Hero is branded.
18.	I	victory	Villain is defeated.
19.	K	liquidation	Initial misfortune or lack is liquidated.
20.	↓	return	Hero returns.
21.	Pr	pursuit, chase	Hero is pursued.
22.	Rs	rescue	Hero is rescued from pursuit.
23.	O	unrecognized arrival	Hero, unrecognized, arrives home or elsewhere.
24.	L	unfounded claims	False hero presents unfounded claims.
25.	M	difficult task	Difficult task is proposed to hero.
26.	N	solution	Task is resolved.
27.	R	recognition	Hero is recognized.
28.	Ex	exposure	False hero or villain is exposed.
29.	T	transfiguration	Hero is given a new appearance.
30.	U	punishment	Villain is punished.
31.	W	wedding	Hero is married, ascends the throne.

While I am on the subject of heroes, let me describe Propp's two kinds of heroes. The first kind, a hero who suffers from the actions of a villain,

TABLE 2.2 Characters and Functions

Kind of Character	Functions
villain	A, H, Pr
donor	D, F
helper	G, K, Rs, N, T
princess (and father)	M, J, Ex, U, W
dispatcher	B
hero	C, E, W
false hero	C, E, L

is what Propp calls a "victim hero" (the focus is on what happens to him); the second kind, a hero who helps others who have suffered some villainy, is what he calls a "seeker hero" (the focus is on the characters helped by the hero). Propp notes that he does not find both kinds of heroes in any one of the fairy tales he analyzes. It is not always easy, I might point out, to determine which kind of heroes or heroines we are dealing with in modern texts—or even in fairy tales.

After listing and discussing his 31 functions, Propp makes a number of what he calls "general inferences," which can be summarized as follows: (a) There are only 31 functions; (b) one function develops out of another logically (not a single function excludes another one); and (c) functions often arrange themselves in pairs (struggle/victory) or in groups (villainy, dispatch, decision for counteraction, departure from home). Propp also suggests, in his discussion of the attributes of characters, that it is possible to identify "one tale with respect to which all fairy tales will appear as variants" (p. 89), and that at the core of fairy tales are certain "abstract representations," which he identifies as myths.

Propp suggests that his functions are distributed in specific ways among the dramatis personae—the characters involved in the stories. Many of the functions logically join together into certain "spheres" that correspond to their respective performers. Table 2.2 shows Propp's main characters and the functions associated with each in a schematized list I have created from the information contained in Propp's chapter titled "The Distributions of Functions Among Dramatis Personae." According to Propp, there are three possible relations between characters and functions: A character takes care of one sphere of action, a character participates in a number of spheres of action, or a sphere of action is split among a number of different characters.

Propp explains that the important thing is what characters do, not what they feel, think they are doing, intend to do, or say they will do. That is, a character's function is crucial, the function being, as I pointed out earlier, the character's actions relative to other main components of the story. Thus, for example, a villain may unwittingly give a magic agent to a hero figure; if this happens, the villain functions as a donor figure.

Propp discusses also a number of other aspects of his theory, such as how characters provide information to one another (a process he calls "notification") and how characters are motivated, but these topics are not of significance for us at this point. *Morphology of the Folktale* remains essential reading for those who are interested in the study of narratives. Propp offers what can be described as a syntagmatic analysis of narratives; a syntagm is a chain, and Propp's analysis focuses on the way a narrative evolves over time, as one narrateme follows another. That is, Propp helps us understand what happens in a story—how plots are structured and the roles of various characters.

In *The Prison-House of Language,* Fredric Jameson (1972) offers an interesting insight about Propp's schema:

> What Propp's discovery implies is that every How (the magical agent) always conceals a Who (the donor), that somewhere hidden in the very structure of the story itself stands the human figure of a mediator, even in those more sophisticated forms in which he is concealed beneath more rational motivation. (p. 67)

There is, then, a central figure, "an Other implied," who turns out not to be the princess but the donor figure. Jameson explains this as follows: "The basic interpersonal and dramatic relationship of the narrative tale is therefore neither the head-on direct one of love nor that of hatred and conflict, but rather this lateral relationship of the hero to the ex-centric figure of the donor" (p. 68). This leads Jameson to suggest that Propp's analysis is not really adequate. Jameson is not the only critic to make this point, and in recent years a considerable number of theorists have offered alternative theories of narrative that attempt to deal with narrative in a more comprehensive and satisfactory manner. Despite its limitations,

TABLE 2.3 Polarities in Propp's Functions

Hero	*Villain*
seeks something	hinders hero
suffers from villain's acts	punishes hero
undergoes ordeals	makes hero undergo ordeals
is dispatched	engages in reconnaissance
gets helpers (magic powers)	has henchmen (evil skills)
heroines (rescued)	enchantresses (bewitch heroes)
seeming villainesses	false heroes shown to be evil
love	lust
young (sons)	old (fathers)
handsome	ugly (often grotesque)
individualists	collectivists
imagination, invention	technology, manpower
finds donor figure	hinders finding donor
defeats villain	loses to hero

however, Propp's theory remains one of the most significant attempts ever made to understand how stories work.

But how do we derive meaning from stories? To understand that, we must consider the ideas of the Swiss linguist Ferdinand de Saussure and the French anthropologist Claude Lévi-Strauss. Saussure is generally considered to be one of the founding fathers of the science of signs, semiology. The term means, literally, "words about (the study of) signs." Saussure (1966) offers a crucial insight about how we find meaning in the world: "Concepts are purely differential and defined not by their positive content but negatively by their relations with the other terms of the system" (p. 117). That is, we don't derive meaning from content per se, but from relationships of terms to other terms. "The most precise characteristic" of concepts, he adds, "is in being what the others are not." As Jonathan Culler (1975) explains, "Structuralists have generally followed Jakobson and taken the binary opposition as a fundamental operation of the human mind basic to the production of meaning" (p. 15). That is, when we are dealing with concepts, notions, or ideas, we make sense of them by contrasting them with their opposites. That is why when we read or hear the word *rich*, we automatically contrast it with *poor,* and when we read or hear the word *happy,* we thinks of the word *sad.* If everyone has a great deal of money, *rich* loses its meaning; *rich* means something only in contrast to *poor.*

A Modification of Propp's Theory

I have used Saussure's insight about oppositional concepts to create a variation on Propp's functions that I first sketched out in my book *Popular Culture Genres* (1992). Table 2.3, which displays some of Propp's functions in terms of polar oppositions, is drawn from that book. This method of displaying these functions is useful in making the functions' natures clearer.

Paradigmatic Analysis
of Narrative Texts

We must keep Saussure's theory in mind when we consider the ideas of Lévi-Strauss (1967), who offers what is termed a *paradigmatic* analysis of texts. In essence, a paradigmatic analysis involves examining the binary oppositions that exist in a text and that can be elicited from the text that give it meaning. In such an analysis, attention is focused not on the sequence of events in the text, which is Propp's focus, but on the various oppositional relationships found in the text. A paradigmatic analysis, Lévi-Strauss suggests, reveals what the text means to people, in contrast to a syntagmatic analysis, which is concerned with what happens in a text.

I would like to suggest a modification of Lévi-Strauss's approach in which, instead of a focus on bundles of related elements in a text, attention is devoted to what I would describe as the text's central oppositions—eliciting from a given text a set of binary oppositions that enable us to make sense of it. What we are doing, in effect, is taking Saussure's insight about the differential definitions of concepts and applying it to characters and their actions, to help us understand the meaning of what characters say and do in texts.

TABLE 2.4 Polar Oppositions in "Humpty Dumpty"

safety	danger
stability	unsteadiness
on the ground	on a (high) wall
solid object	liquid in container (egg)
hard to break	very fragile
wholeness	pieces
reconstitution possible	reconstitution impossible

Let us consider "Humpty Dumpty" in this regard. To make sense of this text we must be aware of a set of oppositions—either stated or implied—that tell us what the actions of the characters (the equivalent of concepts in Saussurean terms) mean. We need not consciously think of the oppositions found in a text, but, if Saussure is correct, whenever we encounter any concept, we automatically make sense of it by recognizing, on some level, that it is not its opposite.

> *Humpty Dumpty sat on a wall,*
> *Humpty Dumpty had a great fall;*
> *All the king's horses*
> *And all the king's men*
> *Couldn't put Humpty Dumpty together again.*

What are the oppositions that can be found in this text? First, we can identify the matter of sitting as opposed to standing, and that of being on a wall instead of on the ground. Then we have the great fall, as opposed to a little fall or remaining on the wall and not falling at all. Finally, we have the matter of Humpty Dumpty retaining his form instead of smashing to pieces, and the matter of being able to be put back together as contrasted with not being able to be put back together. We are not actually told that Humpty Dumpty smashes into a number of pieces, but this is implied by the final line. That is the case, of course, because he is an egg (also not mentioned in the narrative, but information available as part of general cultural knowledge). Had he been a different kind of object, the king's horses and men might have been able to put him back together again.

The sets of oppositions that can be found in "Humpty Dumpty" are displayed in Table 2.4; these oppositions can help us make sense of the story. What I suggest is that our minds function like very fast computers, processing all the dialogue and actions of characters and the concepts related to them automatically and unconsciously in terms of their opposites to find meaning in texts. When we submit these texts to analysis, we can elicit the oppositions.

There is some question as to whether the oppositions and other interesting structural relationships that readers find in texts are actually there or are the products of the readers' ingenious imaginations. There are two points of view on this topic, which Dundes (in Propp, 1928/1968) describes as the "hocus-pocus" versus "God's truth" perspectives. One is that what readers elicit from texts is "hocus-pocus," influenced by clever and ingenious critics who "read all kinds of crazy things into" them. The other is that what readers find in texts is "God's truth"; readers do not invent anything but merely point out what is there, though what some readers discover is not or may not be obvious to others.

"Humpty Dumpty," like many nursery rhymes, has some historical relevance. Some have suggested that it alludes to the problems of a particular English king whose armies (the king's horses and king's men) couldn't save his throne. The story also can be interpreted as having a mythological dimension. Humpty Dumpty's fall can be compared with Adam and Eve's great fall from grace, immortality, and innocence, when they were banished from the Garden of Eden. Nothing they did after the fall could repair the harm that had been done, just as nothing could put Humpty Dumpty together again.

Mieke Bal's Distinctions
Among Story, Text, and Fabula

Mieke Bal's *Narratology: Introduction to the Theory of Narrative* (1985) is generally considered to be one of the most important recent or contemporary studies of narrative. I cannot cover all of Bal's ideas here, but I want to discuss a few of her more important ones. In the introduction to *Narratology*, Bal offers a summary and brief definitions of some of the central concepts she uses:

> A *text* is a finite, structured whole composed of language signs. A *narrative text* is a text in which an agent relates a narrative. A *story* is a fabula that is presented in a certain manner. A *fabula* is a series of logically and chronologically related events that are caused or experienced by actors. An *event* is the transition from one state to another state. *Actors* are agents that perform actions. They are not necessarily human. *To act* is defined here as to cause or experience an event. The assertion that a narrative text is one in which a story is related implies that the text is not the story. (p. 5)

Bal explains the difference between a story and a text by using the example of Tom Thumb, a character whose story has been told in many variations. There are many different texts that tell essentially the same story about Tom Thumb, so clearly we cannot equate the story with the texts. Other kinds of stories also exist in many different text forms. For example, there are many different versions of particular jokes. The text is not the same thing as the story.

In a wonderful book titled *Exercises in Style,* Raymond Queneau (1981) illustrates Bal's point well by telling and retelling a very simple little story using 50 or 60 different styles. All of these different texts tell the same story, which concerns a young man with a very long neck who takes an "S" bus in Paris, accuses someone of jostling him, finds a seat, and is then seen a few hours later talking with a friend. Here are sections from a few of Queneau's exercises:

> *Official letter style:* I beg to advise you of the following facts of which I happened to be the equally impartial and horrified witness. Today, at roughly twelve noon, I was present on the platform of a bus which was proceeding up the rue de Courcelles.

> *Cross-examination style:*
>   —At what time did the 12.23 p.m. S-line bus proceeding in the direction of the Porte de Champerret arrive on that day?
>   —At 12:38 p.m.
>   —Were there many people on the aforesaid bus?
>   —Bags of 'em.

> *Dream:* I had the impression that everything was misty and nacreous around me with multifarious and indistinct apparitions, amongst whom however was one figure that stood out fairly clearly, which was that of a young man whose too-long neck . . .

Queneau's book is a clear and brilliant demonstration of the fact that a story can have many different texts.

Bal also discusses the difference between a story and a fabula. The difference concerns the sequence of events (the story), the versions of the story (the texts), and the *"way in which* these events are presented" (the fabulas). As she explains:

> There are, then, three layers found in narratives:
> 1. stories (sequences of events),
> 2. texts (versions of stories), and
> 3. fabulas (a series of logically or chronologically related events that are caused or experienced by actors, the way in which the events are presented). (p. 5)

And that is the point of departure for Bal's discussion of narrative texts. Her book has three main sections, each of which is devoted to one of the three layers enumerated above.

Bal deals with a question that has interested narrative theorists for a long time: Is there a common model, or what might be described as an *ur-model,* upon which all narratives are based and that would enable us to recognize that something is, in fact, a narrative? That is, is there some kind of Platonic "ideal" narrative upon which all narratives are based? Those proposing a Platonic model for narratives employ two arguments. The first suggests that there is a parallelism between the linguistic structure of sentences and that of all narratives; this means that we can see sentences as micronarratives. The second argument is that there is a correspondence between what actors do in narratives and what people do in real life, which suggests that narratives are structured according to the same logical rules and conventional restrictions that order human thought and action. Bal (1985) makes an interesting comment about this argument:

> Everything that can be said about the structure of fabulas also bears on extra-literary facts. Various investigators in this area even refer to themselves as anthropologists or sociologists (e.g., Bremond and Greimas). Consequently, everything that is said about narratives in this chapter should also be applicable to other connected series of human actions as well as to elements in film, theater, news reports, and social and individual events in the world. It would take us too far here to make a statement about such fundamental questions; it is, however, useful to keep in mind

the fact that the theory of *elements* makes describable a segment of reality that is broader than that of narrative texts only. (p. 13)

This statement supports a point I made earlier—that we can take narrative theory and apply it to phenomena that are not literary narratives (that is, not works of imagination, works of art, created texts) but that have narrative elements or structures to them. If "all the world's a stage," then narrative theory can help us to understand the world better and enable us to gain insights we could not obtain any other way.

Seymour Chatman's *Story and Discourse*

The last theorist whose work I will discuss is Seymour Chatman, whose book *Story and Discourse* (1978) is another of the important contemporary analytic studies of narrativity. I will consider only two of Chatman's key points here, starting with his discussion of the fundamental elements of narrative theory:

> Taking poetics as a rationalist discipline, we may ask, as does the linguist about language: what are the necessary components—and only those—of a narrative? Structuralist theory argues that each narrative has two parts: a story (*histoire*), the content or chain of events (actions, happenings), plus what may be called the existents (characters, items of setting); and a discourse (*discours*), that is, the expression, the means by which the content is communicated. In simple terms the story is the *what* in a narrative that is depicted, the discourse is the *how*. (p. 19)

It is the form of the narrative that interests Chatman, not its substance, and his book is devoted to a very detailed and sophisticated discussion of this matter.

One of the more important, and useful, distinctions Chatman makes is between what he calls "kernels" and "satellites." As he explains:

> Narrative events have not only a logic of connection, but a logic of *hierarchy*. Some are more important than others. In the classical narrative, only major events are part of the chain or armature of contingency. Minor events have a different structure. According to Barthes, each such major event—which I call *kernel* . . . is part of the hermeneutic code; it advances the plot by raising and satisfying questions. Kernels are narrative mo-

ments that give rises to cruxes in the direction taken by events. They are nodes or hinges in the structure, branching points which force a movement into one of two (or more) possible paths. Achilles can give up his girl or refuse; Huck Finn can remain at home or set off down the river; Lambert Strether can advise Chad to remain in Paris or to return; Miss Emily can pay the taxes or send the collector packing; and so on. Kernels cannot be deleted without destroying the narrative logic. In the classical narrative text, proper interpretation of events at any given point is a function of the ability to follow these ongoing selections, to see later kernels as consequences of earlier. (pp. 53-54)

Chatman contrasts kernels with what he calls "satellites," which are relatively minor events that occur in narratives. Satellites embellish the kernels, add details to them, and flesh them out, but they are not central to the logic of narratives and can be eliminated without doing damage to the way the plot works itself out. It is the kernels that determine how the plot develops, and they cannot be removed without seriously changing the plot. We can infer the existence of kernels from satellites, but not the other way around. Chatman's distinction between kernels and satellites provides us with a means of looking at narratives and separating the essential components of their plots from secondary matters. We can also apply this distinction to our everyday lives: What are the essentials and what are the frills?

In the chapters that follow, I will discuss some of the basic techniques used by those who create literary and what used to be called subliterary (that is, popular culture) narratives. I will then deal with some of the different kinds of narratives Americans tend to like as they move through their life cycles and the various forms that narratives take in U.S. popular culture and the media in which they are found. This will set the stage for my analysis of the narrative nature of nonliterary or extraliterary phenomena in everyday life. (For those interested in investigating narrative theory in more detail, I recommend investigating some of the works listed in the reference section.)

A Note on Genres

There are an almost infinite number of narratives in the world, but we can categorize them in certain ways so that potential readers (televi-

Narrative Theory
(theories about the nature of narratives of all kinds)
↑
Narrative Genres
(on television, for example: science fiction, westerns, situation comedies,
detective stories, soap operas, news shows, commercials)
↑
Narrative Texts
(all narrative texts that exist)

Figure 2.1. The Ladder of Abstraction

sion viewers, film audiences, theatergoers, and so on) know what to expect. We use the term *genre,* which means "kind," in classifying texts. When we talk about popular culture texts, we generally have in mind popular fiction and mainstream films and television programs.

There is a ladder of abstraction involved in this analysis. On the bottom level we have all the texts (all the comic books, novels, television shows, films, and so on) that are found in the world. On the next higher level, we find genres—our classification system for texts. And on the highest level we have narrative theory, which covers everything below it. The relationships between these levels are shown in Figure 2.1.

Let's take television, for example, as the source of narrative texts. We find a huge number of different genres in this medium, including commercials, news shows, documentaries, situation comedies, action-adventure shows, science-fiction programs, soap operas, talk shows, detective stories, hospital shows, religious programs, and sporting events. All genres follow certain conventions; that is, they are formulaic and have certain kinds of structures. As we are socialized from childhood to adulthood, we absorb the nature of different genres' particular conventions. Narrative genres have heroes, villains, conflicts, and resolutions. They take place in certain time periods and in certain locations. A program's genre classification tells us in general what we can expect from it, though we may not know precisely what will happen.

We seldom think about how many narrative genres there are or about the number of narratives we see in a given day or week of television viewing. Martin Esslin (1982) notes:

On the most obvious level television is a dramatic medium simply because a large proportion of the material it transmits is in the form of traditional drama mimetically represented by actors and employing plot, dialogue, character, gesture, costume—the whole panoply of dramatic means of expression. . . . According to the 1980 edition of *The Media Book*, in the Spring of 1979 American men on average watched television for over 21 hours per week, while the average American woman's viewing time reached just over 25 hours per week. The time devoted by the average American adult male to watching dramatic material on television thus amounts to over 12 hours per week, while the average American woman sees almost 16 hours of drama on television each week. That means the average American adult sees the equivalent of *five to six full-length stage plays a week!* (p. 7)

This is a remarkable figure, if you think about it. As Esslin points out, for a theatergoer to see even one play a week is an achievement.

Television is, in large measure, a dramatic or, for purposes of this discussion, narrative medium. Many of the programs on television, although not "dramas" (by which Esslin means narrative fictions), have dramatic structure or narrative elements in them. I will return to this subject in later chapters, after I discuss narrative techniques.

If I am told (in *Goldfinger*) that *Bond saw a man of about fifty*, the piece of information holds simultaneously two functions of unequal pressure: on the one hand, the character's age fits into a certain description of the man (the "usefulness" of which for the rest of the story is not nil, but diffuse, delayed); while on the other, the immediate signified of the statement is that Bond is unacquainted with his future interlocutor, the unit thus implying a very strong correlation (initiation of a threat and the need to establish the man's identity). In order to determine the initial narrative units, it is therefore vital never to lose sight of the functional nature of the segments under consideration and to recognize in advance that they will not necessarily coincide with the forms into which we traditionally cast the various parts of narrative discourse (actions, scenes, paragraphs, dialogues, interior monologues, etc.) still less with "psychological" divisions (modes of behavior, feelings, intentions, motivations, rationalizations or characters).

Roland Barthes, *Image-Music-Text* (1977, pp. 90-91)

3

Narrative Techniques and Authorial Devices

How are narratives created? In this chapter I will discuss some of the devices and techniques that authors (and, by extension, creative artists working in all media) use when they create narrative texts. When we read narrative texts, we are usually interested primarily in the stories being related; we seldom think about the various devices or "tricks" the authors use to tell those stories, but, as you will see, there are many.

In an essay titled "Art as Technique," the Russian literary theorist Victor Shklovsky (1989) argues that works of art "defamiliarize" people and present the world in ways with which they are not familiar, ways they are unaccustomed to. He also discusses the various devices writers use in creating texts. "In art," according to Shklovsky, "it is our experience of the process of construction that counts, not the finished product" (quoted in Scholes, 1974, p. 84). The term *devices* may seem somewhat strange in this context, because when one reads a good novel, for example, everything flows along very smoothly, generally speaking, and the reader is unaware of the "art" that has gone into creating the text.

Authors do use a number of different methods to accomplish their aims, however, and that is what I wish to discuss here—the process of construction by which the creators of narrative texts generate their effects. I cannot deal with all authorial devices within the confines of this chapter, but I will consider a number of the more important ones. In so doing, I am discussing the art of the narrative, the numerous ways in which authors convey information to their readers as a means of shaping the readers' thoughts and affecting their emotions.

A Gloss on Propp's Functions

Let me start by returning to the modifications I made to Propp's (1928/1968) theory in my book *Popular Culture Genres* (1992). In addition to offering Propp's main functions in a set of bipolar oppositions, I also dealt with Propp's notions about who the main characters are in fairy tales, what their basic actions are, and what their goals are. These topics are expressed here in Tables 3.1, 3.2, and 3.3, which also use bipolar oppositions.

We start with the basic actions of characters in Table 3.1. This table, which takes the form of a list of polar oppositions, covers many of the actions of characters in narrative texts (it is impossible to deal with everything a character might do, of course). Although in real life we are capable of doing all kinds of things, from traveling to the North Pole to shooting people, most of us, fortunately, limit our activities to a relatively narrow range of activities. In fiction, on the other hand, anything and everything is possible.

We move on in Table 3.2 to the goals of heroes and villains and the kinds of things they do in typical fairy tales and, by extension, all kinds of modernizations of fairy tales. These goals are taken from Propp; they are very limited in number and pitched at an extremely high level of abstraction. When we deal with modern texts we have to interpret these goals very broadly, but they are useful for analyzing what motivates characters in a large number of narratives.

Finally, we move on to Propp's notions about the major characters found in fairy tales (Table 3.3). We also have to update and modernize these characters, but they offer an overview of common character types found in texts.

TABLE 3.1 Basic Actions of Characters in Fairy Tales

cooperate	versus	compete
help	versus	hinder
escape	versus	imprison
defend	versus	attack
initiate	versus	respond
disguise	versus	uncover
pretend	versus	reveal
love	versus	hate
unravel	versus	mystify
pursue	versus	evade
search for	versus	evade
tell truth	versus	lie
allow	versus	prohibit
question	versus	answer
rescue	versus	endanger
protect	versus	threaten
suffer	versus	punish
dispatch	versus	summon
allow	versus	interdict
retain	versus	lose

My point in presenting these tables is to suggest that when we follow the exploits of characters, we see and interpret everything they do in terms of bipolar oppositions (generally not recognized or brought to awareness by the reader) that give any action meaning. Some of the oppositions given as examples here may be a bit forced, but they give a sense of how our minds work when we read texts—if, that is, Saussure

TABLE 3.2 Goals of Heroes and Villains in Fairy Tales

Goals of Heroes	*Goals of Villains*
overcome a villain	overcome a hero
rescue a victim	kidnap a victim
succeed in a quest or task	prevent hero from succeeding
make up for a lack	create a lack
freedom	enslavement

TABLE 3.3 Opposing Types Among Primary Characters Found in Fairy
                Tales

heroes	villains
helpers	henchmen
princesses (love objects)	sirens (sexual objects)
magicians (good magic)	sorcerers (evil magic)
donors of magic objects	preventers/hinderers of donors
dispatchers of heroes	captors of heroes
seekers	avoiders
seeming villains who are good	false heroes/heroines who are evil

(1966) and Jakobson (1985) are correct about the mind's finding meaning in things by setting up bipolar oppositions (generally without our awareness, of course). There are some critics, I should point out, who argue that this matter of setting up bipolar oppositions is questionable, and that the oppositions that are elicited don't really hold up when scrutinized.

Devices Authors Use
to Convey Information

Let me now turn to some commonly used authorial devices—techniques authors use to convey information to readers, either directly or indirectly (by having characters convey information to one another). I will use for examples primarily two classic detective stories, *Murder on the Orient Express*, by Agatha Christie (1940), and *The Maltese Falcon*, by Dashiell Hammett (1930/1972), though I will use some other narrative texts as well.

Authors often speak to readers in indirect ways. When authors offer descriptions, through their choices of nouns, verbs, adverbs, and adjectives they are actually speaking to readers, telling them what they should think about certain characters or events. Descriptions and the figurative language found in them (and the other techniques authors use) give readers considerable amounts of information, as we shall see shortly.

Readers must always keep in mind that, as Yuri Lotman (1977) has noted, nothing that happens in a text is irrelevant or accidental. This point has also been made by Aristotle, as a matter of fact; he suggests that if we take one thing out of a well-constructed work, it will suffer. A great deal of what authors do when they write stems from their psyches and functions at an unconscious level, so often writers can't explain why they used this word rather than that one or had a character do X instead of Y. That is the task of critics.

Many of the devices found in popular literary works can also be found in narratives in other media, such as film and television, though sometimes the devices take somewhat different form—for example, what we can see on the screen in a movie takes the place of a written description. In some cases devices are used in tandem, so that, for example, we get a summary that is also a confession, but it is usually possible to determine which device is basic. I will discuss below in turn the following common authorial devices:

- Descriptions
- Thoughts of characters
- Dialogue
- Summaries
- Characterization
- Stereotypes
- Overheard conversations
- Letters, telegrams, and other correspondence
- Articles from publications
- Phone calls
- Confessions

Descriptions

Descriptions are one of the most important means through which authors give us information. They tell us what characters look like and how they behave, help situate actions, and generate feelings and attitudes in readers. Let me offer an example from *The Maltese Falcon*. Sam Spade, who has entered the apartment of Caspar Gutman, describes what Gutman looks like as Gutman comes to greet him:

The fat man was flabbily fat with bulbous pink cheeks and lips and chins and neck, with a great soft egg of a belly that was all his torso, and

pendant cones for arms and legs. . . . all his bulbs rose and shook and fell
separately with each step, in the manner of clustered soap bubbles not
yet released from the pipe through which they had been blown. (p. 108)

Gutman, we are told, is dressed in a cutaway coat and wears an ascot
anchored by a pink pearl stickpin. Hammett later describes Gutman's
voice as having a "throaty purr" to it.

This is a marvelous piece of writing that gives the reader a very
precise picture of the aptly named Caspar Gutman (gut + man) and a
sense of what he is like. Notice Hammett's use of metaphor. The "flabbily
fat" Gutman's stomach is "a great soft egg," and when he moves his
body, it shakes "in the manner of clustered soap bubbles." These descriptions help the reader form a fairly precise picture of Gutman.

Description, we can see, can be used for more than creating a visual
image; description can also suggest character, personality, and many
other things as well. We infer a great deal from the way people look—
from the shapes of their bodies, from their body language, from their
eyes, from the clothes that they wear, from their hairstyles. (Can we see
Gutman as, perhaps, a modernized kind of Humpty Dumpty figure, who
is also going to have a "great fall"?)

Thoughts

By telling their readers what characters are thinking, authors can
provide important information about such matters as what has happened in the plot (that is, summaries) and ideas a character may have
about various other characters and what is motivating them.

In *Murder on the Orient Express,* a passenger on the Orient Express named Ratchett has been murdered in a puzzling way. Christie has her detective, Hercule Poirot, lay out the possibilities regarding Ratchett's murder. Then Christie cuts to a chapter that includes, among other things, the thoughts of one of the main characters, Monsieur Bouc. He is an officer of the Orient Express railroad company and a friend of Poirot, who at the last moment has secured him a place on the train (in a cabin next to Ratchett's, by chance). Christie has Bouc indulge in speculation about who might have murdered Ratchett (using highly stereotyped thinking) and gives us yet another hint about the role of one of the passengers, a young Englishwoman named Mary Debenham, in the affair. Christie tells us that Bouc is thinking about the murder and who might have done it:

> Poirot obviously thinks that this English girl is mixed up in the matter. I cannot help feeling that this is most unlikely. . . . The English are extremely cold. Probably it is because they have no figures. . . . But that is not the point. It seems like the Italian could not have done it—a pity. I suppose the English valet is not lying when he said the other never left the compartment? But should he? It is not easy to bribe the English; they are so unapproachable. (p. 204)

After telling the reader what Bouc is thinking, Christie moves on to what another character, Dr. Constantine, is thinking and then to other things. Such passages, in which the author tells the reader what characters are thinking, are useful devices for planting ideas in readers' minds.

From a technical standpoint, Christie functions as an "omniscient narrator," one who can tell what is in the minds of various characters in addition to describing them and showing them in action. One of the cardinal rules in writing is to "show, not tell," but in some cases it is useful to be able to tell, and displaying the thoughts of characters is a common way of doing so.

Visual media usually use more indirect ways of showing what people are thinking—through flashbacks and facial expressions, for instance. It is also possible to show what characters are thinking by having them record their thoughts in diaries, letters, journals (on paper or on disk), and so on.

Dialogue

Dialogue is the most common means by which characters convey information to one another and, at the same time, indirectly to readers. What characters say to one another allows readers to gain insight into their personalities and thoughts and to gain information about their actions. Novelists also use dialogue to create distinctive personalities; if all the characters in a novel sound the same, the reader can become confused and bored. Consider this passage from *Murder on the Orient Express* in which Hercule Poirot is chatting with Bouc as they are dining. Bouc sighs, "If I had but the pen of Balzac! . . ." and adds:

> "All around us are people, of all classes, of all nationalities, of all ages. For three days these people, these strangers to one another, are brought together. They sleep and eat under one roof, they cannot get away from one another. At the end of three days they part, they go their several ways, never perhaps to see each other again."
>
> "And yet," said Poirot, "suppose an accident—"
>
> "Ah, no, my friend—"
>
> "From your point of view it would be regrettable, I agree. But nevertheless let us just for one moment suppose it. Then, perhaps, all these people here are linked together—by death." (pp. 29-30)

This bit of dialogue is of central importance to the story, for Christie is really giving away the main point of the mystery—which is that *all* of the people on the train *are* linked together by death (by one death that occurred in the past and one that is to occur), though most readers probably miss this point. Christie then turns her readers' attention away from Poirot's speculations and discounts them by having Bouc suggest that Poirot may have indigestion.

Notice the way Christie has created her dialogue. Bouc "sighed" when he talks about Balzac. Then she uses the simple verb *said* to describe Poirot's response to Bouc. Later on, Christie dispenses with any kind of verb and just has Bouc speak: "Ah, no, my friend—" Then Poirot answers, "I agree," echoing an earlier use by Bouc of the word *agree*.

Words such as *said* and *agree* convey different ideas. There are many other verbs authors use in describing how dialogue is conducted, and all of them convey different feelings and meanings. Consider, for example, the following list of some of the verbs that may accompany dialogue:

- said
- snarled
- replied
- answered
- announced
- asserted
- screamed
- hissed
- exploded
- agreed
- responded
- retorted
- decreed
- whispered
- whined
- told

Each of these generates a different feeling, gives the reader a different notion about what a character feels or is like and the relationships that exist between and among characters. Table 3.4 lists some of these words and gives some corresponding possible meanings. Authors can create attitudes in the minds of their readers by something as simple as their choice of words to introduce or conclude a bit of dialogue. And the dialogue itself is always revelatory.

TABLE 3.4 Implied Meanings of Verbs Used With Dialogue

Verb	Implied Meaning
whispered	secrecy, intimacy
shrieked	excitement, anger, fear
exploded	rage
agreed	consensus, accord
asked	questioning
hissed	menace (snakelike)
intimated	suggestion, hinting
announced	public nature of response
whined	complaining, whimpering

There is a subcategory of dialogue that I would describe as interrogation, in which, for example, a detective questions suspects and others to gain information. Notice how economically Agatha Christie does this in *Murder on the Orient Express* as Hercule Poirot questions another character:

> "The train had stopped then?"
> "The train had stopped."
> "You heard nothing—nothing unusual during the time, Madame?"
> "I heard nothing unusual."
> "What is your maid's name?"
> "Hildegarde Schmidt."
> "She has been with you long?"
> "Fifteen years." (pp. 115-116)

Note that when the two characters are well delineated, it is possible to dispense with everything but the dialogue itself.

During his interrogations, Poirot learns all kinds of things that are intended to seem trivial and irrelevant to the reader but that provide Poirot with the information he needs to solve the crime. Mystery writers purposely bury their clues in descriptions and dialogue. At the ends of their stories, when they explain their reasoning, readers can see that they ignored important information that was given to them that would have enabled them to solve the crime before the detective did. Mystery stories are often called "whodunits," and part of the charm of this genre lies in trying to solve the crime before the detective does—figuring out "whodunit."

Summaries

At various stages in the average detective story (and in narrative texts in general) the author provides summaries in which what has gone on so far is reviewed in a highly abbreviated manner. This is necessary to help readers keep track of things, to condense certain activities, and sometimes to indicate that certain things have happened without having to dramatize them or have characters act them out. Summaries also can be used by the author to interpret events in the text for the reader.

For example, in *Dr. No* (1958), one of Ian Fleming's James Bond spy stories, Fleming uses a summary to recount Dr. No's history and explain how he has come to look the way he does. No explains how some killers came and cut off his hands and tried to shoot him through the heart, but No was not killed because his heart is on the right side of his body, not the left. No continues with his history, talking about how he has changed the way he looks:

> I had all my hair taken out by the roots, my thick nose made thin, my mouth widened, my lips sliced. I could not get smaller, so I made myself taller. I wore built up shoes. I had weeks of traction on my spine. I held myself differently. I put away my mechanical hands and wore hands of wax inside gloves. I changed my name to Julius No—the Julius after my father and the No for my rejection of him and all authority. I threw away my spectacles and wore contact lenses. (p. 138)

No continues for a while, mentioning that he purchased Crab Key island and has been there for 14 years. "I was entertained," he adds, "by the idea of converting bird dung into gold" (p. 139).

This summary provides the reader with an understanding of what Dr. No's past has been like, explains something about his personality and motivations, and sets the stage for the remainder of the action in the novel—which concludes by having Bond survive an ordeal and, fittingly, kill Dr. No by dumping a load of guano on him.

Sometimes summaries are contained in dialogue. Because their basic function is to summarize, I include these under the category of summaries rather than dialogue. Let me offer an example from *The Maltese Falcon*. At the end of the book, Spade is talking with Brigid O'Shaugnessy and gives his reading of various events that have recently transpired:

> You came into my bed to stop me asking questions. You led me out yesterday for Gutman with that phony call for help. Last night you came here with them and waited outside for me and came in with me. You were in my arms when the trap was sprung—I couldn't have gone for a gun if I'd had one on me and couldn't have made a fight if I wanted to. (p. 224)

In this bit of dialogue, Spade is recapitulating recent events in the book, but he is doing more than that: He is characterizing Brigid and establishing himself as a person who, unlike most of the other men she has dealt with in her career, is unwilling to "play the sap" for her.

Characterization

A great deal of characterization is accomplished through description and dialogue, as well as through action. Two of the pillars of characterization are the author's description of (a) what a character looks like and is like and (b) how a character behaves. Through characters' actions, readers get a sense of what they are like by interpreting those actions according to the readers' own moral codes and value systems.

Consider, for example, the way Christie describes Ratchett in *Murder on the Orient Express.* Poirot is having dinner at a hotel in Istanbul and, while scanning the restaurant, notices a man of between 60 and 70 years old talking with a younger companion. At first glance, the man seems to have a kindly look about him:

> His slightly bald head, his domed forehead, the smiling mouth that displayed a very white set of false teeth—all seemed to speak of a benevolent personality. Only the eyes belied this assumption. They were small, deep-set and crafty. Not only that. As the man, making some remark to his companion, glanced across the room, his gaze stopped on Poirot for a moment and just for that second there was a strange malevolence, an unnatural tensity in the glance.
>
> Then he rose.
>
> "Pay the bill, Hector," he said.
>
> His voice was slightly husky in tone. It had a queer, soft, dangerous quality. (p. 23)

Christie characterizes Ratchett in the most negative tones, using such words as "malevolence," "unnatural," "queer," and "dangerous." We later find out that Ratchett is actually the notorious kidnapper Cassetti, who years ago kidnapped a child (an allusion to the Lindbergh case) and killed her, and this led to all kinds of horrendous things and ruined the lives of a number of people. Thus, at the end of the book, when Poirot offers two scenarios to the police—one suggests that every person on the train participated in a ritual killing of Ratchett/Cassetti and the other suggests that a mysterious stranger, who had been described by several of the characters as being on the train for a short while, did it—we are ready to accept the notion that the stranger did it, despite the fact that we actually know who murdered Ratchett.

Some of the things an author may include in describing a character include the following characteristics:

- name
- age
- gender
- height
- weight
- race
- hair color
- hairstyle
- complexion
- eyes
- nose
- posture
- body language
- voice
- accent
- clothes
- facial expression
- occupation
- setting

Often characterization is accomplished through the things characters reveal things about themselves, as in this famous scene in *The Maltese Falcon* in which Brigid O'Shaugnessy pleads with Sam Spade for help:

> Her face was wan, taut, and fearful over tight-clasped hands. "I haven't lived a good life," she cried. "I've been bad—worse than you could know—but I'm not all bad. Look at me. Mr. Spade. You know I'm not all bad, don't you? You can see that, can't you? Then can't you trust me a little? Oh, I'm so alone and afraid, and I've got nobody to help me if you won't help me. I know I've no right to ask you to trust me if I won't trust you. (pp. 35-36)

Brigid's description of herself offers readers a sense of who she is. She admits that she's done some bad things but pleads for Spade's trust.

What the reader doesn't know yet, of course, is that Brigid is, among other things, a cold-blooded killer.

We need characterization to explain motivation, to understand why it is that characters do what they do. There should be a logic to narrative texts, and readers must be convinced that what characters do is plausible, which means their actions must be connected to their personalities and desires. That is, the behavior of characters must be justified somehow so that the reader can accept what happens as logical and reasonable.

Stereotypes

Stereotypes are, for purposes of this discussion, ideas people share about what various groups or categories of people are like. We employ stereotypes in thinking about members of various ethnic and racial groups, occupational groups, genders, socioeconomic classes, and nationalities, among other things. Thus we talk about Mexicans, Jews, Scots, African Americans, Asians, lawyers, gays, members of the upper class, Americans, the French, the English, Russians, and so on, as though all members of these groups are alike. Stereotypes are generally negative, though they can be positive or mixed. Semiotically speaking, stereotypes are metonymies and, more specifically, synecdoches: On the basis of a part (a few people we may have met or have been told about), we make generalizations about the whole.

Although stereotyping is simplistic and often dangerous, it is part of our everyday illogical and uncritical thinking. We apply Ronald Reagan's notion that "if you've seen one redwood, you've seen them all" to people; if you've seen, met, had contact with one Mexican, Jew, African American, or whatever, you know what "they" are like. Despite its illogicality, stereotyping is often used in narrative texts because it allows authors to provide motivations and to characterize people very quickly and economically.

Thus in Ian Fleming's *Dr. No*, which is full of people of different social classes and nationalities, we find a number of stereotypes. Excerpts from the novel containing a number of them are listed below, admittedly taken out of context. James Bond has been sent to Jamaica to investigate the disappearance of a couple of agents. He is taken to lunch by the British colonial secretary, one Pleydell-Smith, who we are told is a graduate of King's College at Cambridge University and a person with strong views about the various ethnic and racial groups who live on Jamaica. All the comments below are made by this character, who is delving beneath the surface of life in Jamaica:

> The Jamaican is a kindly lazy man with the virtues and vices of a child. He lives on a very rich island but he doesn't get rich from it. He doesn't know how to and he's too lazy.

> It's the Portuguese Jews who make the most [money]. They came here with the British and they've stayed. But they're snobs and they spend too much of their fortunes on building fine houses and giving dances.

> Then come the Syrians, very rich too, but not such good businessmen. They have most of the stores and some of the best hotels. They're not a very good risk. Get overstocked and have to have an occasional fire to get liquid again.

> Then there are the Indians, with their usual flashy trade in soft goods and the like. They're not much of a lot.

> Finally there are the Chinese, solid, compact, discreet—the most powerful clique in Jamaica. They've got the bakeries and the laundries and the best food stores. They keep to themselves and keep their strain pure. . . . Not that they don't take the black girls when they want them. You can see the result all over Kingston—Chigroes—Chinese negroes and negresses. The Chigroes are a tough, forgotten race. They look down on the negroes and the Chinese look down on them. One day they may become a nuisance. They've got some of the intelligence of the Chinese and most of the vices of the black man. (pp. 51-52)

These stereotypes suggest that there are strong elements of racism and anti-Semitism in Fleming, who uses a character to express Fleming's antipathies. The same thing is apparent in Christie's work, though not quite as strident. *Murder on the Orient Express* is full of stereotypes of Italians, Americans, Eastern Europeans, and the British. Christie uses her stereotypes of the British as rational and unemotional to give her readers a very important hint (to which most readers probably pay no attention) when she has Poirot say that the mind behind the killing on the Orient Express must be logical and rational and then say to Mary Debenham, a short while later, that she is very Anglo-Saxon, a person who doesn't approve of emotion.

All of these stereotypes are used by Christie to give readers ideas about the characters involved in the murder, though these ideas are often used to lead readers astray. In murder mysteries, one of the standard devices is to offer a number of "red herrings" to throw suspicion on a number of different characters and provide motivations and opportunity for these characters to have done the murder. Christie, an educated and sophisticated woman, used these stereotypes, including the stereotype of the British as cold and reserved; it is hard to know whether she actually held them.

The devices and techniques discussed above are some of the more common ones authors use to communicate information to their readers directly. That is, when authors describe something for their readers, they are, so to speak, addressing them directly and providing information that the authors want the readers to have. In the case of dialogue, of course, the characters are providing information to one another, and the address-ees are the characters, not the readers, though readers also get the information the authors want them to have.

I will now turn to discussion of the techniques that authors use to allow their characters to learn information and, in some cases, to pass this information on to others, what Propp (1928/1968) calls "notifica-tion." I have already discussed dialogue—when two or more characters speak and exchange information, which I define broadly to cover also things like feelings and attitudes.

I will be discussing techniques such as letters, overheard conversa-tions, phone calls, articles in publications, thoughts, and confessions. One could add high-technology analogues: messages on phone re-corders and material on videotapes and computers disks, for instance.

Overheard Conversations

In *Murder on the Orient Express* there is a scene in which the train to Istanbul has made a stop. Poirot is out stretching his legs when he overhears two indistinct figures talking:

"Mary—"
The girl interrupted him.
"Not now. Not now. When it's all over. When it's behind us—*then*—"
(p. 18)

When he hears this Poirot turns away, wondering about what he has heard. He does not recognize Miss Debenham's cool and efficient voice at that moment. Poirot has overheard Miss Debenham speaking with Colonel Arbuthnot and has gained some information of importance—they are not two people who have just met and whose relationship is the casual one as it seemed earlier, when Poirot saw them having a meal together on the train.

Letters

Letters, telegrams, journals, diaries, and other forms of written material allow authors to provide information of importance to characters. In *Murder on the Orient Express* we find that Ratchett has received several letters. The first one goes as follows:

> *Thought you'd double-cross us and get away with it, did you? Not on your life. We're out to GET you, Ratchett, and we WILL get you.* There was no signature.

There is a second letter, similar to the first, threatening Ratchett. It turns out that the letters have not been written by one person, but by a number of people, each person printing one letter at a time. The style of the letters suggests gangsters who are going to get revenge on Ratchett for having double-crossed them.

Christie is giving us another hint here; the letter was written by a group of people—an important bit of information. What cracks the case open, actually, is a scrap of paper Poirot rescues from a fire in Ratchett's apartment; the paper has three words on it, and part of a fourth: "—*member little Daisy Armstrong*" (p. 71). This tells Poirot who the dead man is and sets the stage for him to determine who murdered Ratchett—and why he had to leave the United States. This scrap of paper ultimately enables Poirot to figure out that everyone on the train is connected, one way or another, with Daisy Armstrong's family and to solve the crime.

Articles From Publications

Hammett makes use of a clipping from a San Francisco newspaper in *The Maltese Falcon*. Spade has found a newspaper in Joel Cairo's room with a segment torn out of it:

> Spade went to the Business Office of the *Call*, bought a copy of the previous day's issue, opened it to the shipping-news page, and compared it with the page taken from Cairo's wastebasket. The missing portion had read:
>
> > *5:17 a.m.—Tahiti from Sydney to Papeete.*
> > *6:03 a.m.—Admiral Peoples from Astoria.*
> > *8:07 a.m.—Caddopeak from San Pedro.*
> > *8:17 a.m.—Silverado from San Pedro.*
> > *8:25 a.m.—La Paloma from Hong Kong.*
> > *9:03 a.m.—Daisy Gray from Seattle.*
>
> He read the list slowly and when he had finished he underscored *Hong Kong* with a fingernail, cut the list of arrivals from the paper with his pocket-knife, put the rest of the paper and Cairo's sheet into the wastebasket, and returned to his office. (p. 143)

This information from the newspaper introduces the ship *La Paloma*, whose captain happens to be carrying the Maltese Falcon and who delivers it to Spade before dying of gunshot wounds. We are able to follow the way Spade's mind is working and get information of value—though as readers we can't be sure what the full significance is of the information Spade has obtained.

Phone Calls

Phone calls are another useful way for authors to provide information; they can also serve other functions, for example, as transitions from one scene or event to another. Thus Chapter 11 of *The Maltese Falcon* begins with a phone call from Gutman to Spade. Gutman invites Spade to come see him in 15 minutes:

> The telephone-bell was ringing when Spade returned to his office after sending Brigid O'Shaugnessy off to Effie Perine's house. He went to the

telephone. "Hello. . . . Yes, this is Spade. . . . Yes, I got it. I've been waiting to hear from you. (p. 105)

In this particular conversation, we do not "hear" the voice of Gutman but we can make out, via the ellipses, the nature of the conversation. It is, of course, possible for authors to show both sides of a conversation, if that suits their purposes.

What this conversation does is move the action along; it provides a way for Hammett to introduce Gutman into the action and generates a meeting between them. It is at this meeting that Hammett offers the wonderful description of Gutman quoted earlier. With the development of modern technology, we now can have characters using phones in their automobiles, on boats, on airplanes, and so on. And we also have beepers and other kinds of personal communications devices that can serve the same function in narratives as ordinary phone calls. All of these devices can be used to convey information to one or more of the characters and thus indirectly to readers.

Confessions

At the end of *Murder on the Orient Express* we find Linda Arden, the grandmother of Daisy Armstrong, who has pretended to be Mrs. Hubbard (one the characters involved in Ratchett's murder), confessing. She explains that everyone who had suffered from the Armstrong kidnapping had agreed that Cassetti had to be killed. They had considered drawing lots, but the chauffeur Antonio suggested that everyone participate in the killing and Mary Debenham and Hector MacQueen figured out how it might be done. This confession explains why Ratchett/Cassetti was murdered and how the murderers went about planning the killing. It also justifies the murder, as we learn that Cassetti had bought his way out of a conviction somehow, and suggests that, in reality, justice was being done.

Linda Arden adds, a bit later: "There had been other children kidnapped before Daisy, and there might be others in the future. Society had condemned him—we were only carrying out the sentence" (p. 255). Given this situation, there is good reason for Poirot to propose a scenario suggesting that Ratchett was killed by a mysterious stranger as plausible and letting Bouc and the others decide what to tell the police.

Most confessions in murder mysteries are not like this one; usually the murderer, having been exposed, explains why or how he or she did the murder, and that wraps up the story very neatly. In some cases where it is impossible to prove who did the killing, a confession is used to catch the murderer. In such stories the murderer usually thinks he or she has the detective or another person in his or her power; feeling safe, the murderer explains why and how he or she did the murder. This explanation, which functions as a confession, is overheard by the police, who then come in and arrest the murderer.

Conclusion

We can see that a good deal of storytelling relies on authors' transmitting information to readers directly (through descriptions, summaries, stereotypes, and other means) or indirectly (by having characters transmit information to one another through dialogue, letters, phone calls, and so on). We can think of such techniques as devices that authors use to generate certain effects in readers. Texts are not simple, natural matters, but complex works that achieve their effects as the result of authors' skills in blending action, dialogue, and characterization and offering information of various kinds to readers.

When we read a detective story—or any narrative, for that matter—we may be intrigued by the complexity of the plot, but we should also be aware of the numerous devices and techniques the author uses to achieve his or her ends. The degree to which we are unaware of the use of these devices is one of the marks of a good writer.

Nothing . . . is more possible than that [the novelist] be of a turn of mind for which this odd literal opposition of description and dialogue, incident and description, has little meaning and light. People often talk of these things as if they had a kind of internecine distinctness, instead of melting into each other at every breath, and being intimately associated parts of one general effort of expression. I cannot imagine composition existing in a series of blocks, nor conceive, in any novel worth discussing at all, of a passage of dialogue that is not in its intention descriptive, a touch of truth of any sort that does not partake of the nature of incident, or an incident that derives its interest from any other source than the general and only source of success of a work of art—that of being illustrative. A novel is a living thing, all one and continuous, like any other organism, and in proportion as it lives it will be found, I think, that in each of the parts there is something of each of the other parts.

Henry James, *The Art of the Novel*
(1934, quoted in Tzvetan Todorov, 1981, p. 9)

4

A Glossary of Terms
Relating to Narrative Texts

This chapter consists of a glossary of terms used in the discussion to this point as well as some others of significance. This will provide a comprehensive overview of narrative theory and function as a resource for those who may wish to find definitions of various aspects of narratives. My definitions are drawn from the works cited as well as a number of other works, such as M. H. Abrams's *A Glossary of Literary Terms* (1988) and Sylvan Barnet, Morton Berman, and William Burto's *A Dictionary of Literary Terms* (1960).

Action: The events that take place in a narrative; what characters do. "To act is . . . to cause or experience an event" (Bal, 1985, p. 5). It is through a character's actions (as well as what the character says) that we get a sense of the kind of person he or she is. *Action* also is used to describe narratives in which there is a high level of physical activity. The television genre of action-adventure comprises shows in which there is a great deal of movement—chases, physical conflict (fighting and other violence), and so on. The events take place one after another, at a very rapid pace.

Allegory: A metaphorical story that has symbolic significance, with implications beyond the story itself. Allegories tie together themes and ideas of a broad philosophical nature and convey some kind of a moral. The television series *The Prisoner* provides an example. This series involves a spy who has resigned from that profession and is subsequently imprisoned on a mysterious island, deprived of his name and given a new "designation" (Number 6); he has various adventures in which he fights with the administrators of the island and tries to escape. Eventually, he destroys the island and escapes. This series can be seen as an allegory illustrating the triumph of the human spirit and democratic individualism over the forces of totalitarian bureaucracy and adversity in general.

Characterization: The ways in which the personalities and motivations of characters are portrayed through description, action, dialogue, and so on.

Characters: The people found in a story who do the actions that lead to the resolution of the story (Bal, 1985, uses the term "actors"). Readers must find characters interesting and want to follow their adventures, so authors have to find ways of making characters worth bothering with, so to speak. As a rule, the characters in narratives are not representative of ordinary people. On television, for example, there are proportionally many more police officers, detectives, and killers than there are in real life, and many fewer blue-collar workers. Many narrative theorists argue that character is the basis of action in narratives, whereas others argue that action reveals character.

Climax or **Crisis:** The turning point of a story, when the most important matter is somehow decided, setting the stage for the resolution of the story. Every story must have a climax, must lead to some kind of resolution that readers (ideally) find interesting and satisfying.

Complication: The introduction of opposition and conflict into a story after the exposition. Sometimes a complication is internal and involves a character who is torn between two choices, each of which is problematic. In other cases, good guys (or good women) are opposed by bad guys (or bad women) and the complication is easily recognized.

Dramatic irony: A state that occurs when a story resolves itself in ways not anticipated (and generally the opposite of what is desired) by a particular character. When a character who thinks he will victimize another character turns out to be victimized by that character instead, for example, there is dramatic irony.

Episode: A scenario or scene in which an action takes place. A plot needs a number of episodes to allow for adequate development, for rising and falling action, for conflict, and for satisfying resolutions. For televised serial texts, such as soap operas and situation comedies, *episode* refers to a segment broadcast in a particular week.

Event: An incident within a story that provides for "transition from one state to another state" (Bal, 1985). An event is something that happens in a text that leads to something else happening and, ultimately, to the resolution of the story.

Fabula: "A series of logically and chronologically related events that are caused or experienced by actors" (Bal, 1985, p. 6).

Formula: A highly conventional scheme used in a text, involving stock characters and recognizable plot structures. Genre texts such as westerns, science fiction stories, detective stories, and romances are often highly formulaic. They take place in certain kinds of locations and have specific kinds of characters who engage in predictable kinds of actions. If we can imagine a continuum between texts that are highly conventional and ones that are highly inventive, formulaic texts would be found very close to the conventional end of the continuum. Some publishers of romances, for example, publish guidelines for authors that specify such things as the ages of heroes and heroines, what they should look like, whether or not either or both can be divorced (and, if so, how long before the action of the story the divorce has to have taken place), whether or not they can have sex before marriage, and so on.

Frame: A story that provides the means of telling other stories within it. For example, in *Rashomon*, Kurosawa's classic film, a group of men take shelter from rain in a temple, where they discuss an outrageous incident that has occurred. It seems that a bandit has been captured who has tied up a man, had sex with the man's wife in front of him (was it rape or seduction?), and may have killed the man. The men in the temple provide a frame for the plot as they discuss conflicting versions of what went on. These versions, given by each of the characters involved, are told in flashbacks. Frames are very useful in plots that have a serial nature and contain a number of stories, such as *1,001 Arabian Nights*.

Exposition or **Rising action:** Information provided to the reader about what is going on; characters are introduced and readers get a sense of what their relationships are. The action "rises" until there is some crisis, after which it recedes and a resolution to the story is provided.

Flashback: A return in a story to events that took place at an earlier period than the one being presented; also known as *retrospect*. Flashbacks help readers get a sense of what happened earlier that led to the present situation and what motivates characters.

Jeopardy: Danger; characters who are in danger of some kind are said to be in jeopardy. Placing characters in jeopardy is a device used to create interest and suspense in readers. For example, in *Murder on the Orient Express*, Ratchett/Cassetti is in jeopardy; he has received letters threatening him with death. The 12 murderers of Ratchett/Cassetti are also in jeopardy. The question is, Will Poirot find out who murdered Ratchett/Cassetti? And when he does, what will he do?

Motivation: The reasons characters behave as they do. We want characters to behave in logical ways, not just do things randomly. That is, they have to have adequate reasons to do what they do, to support their behavior— they have to have good motives for their acts.

Narrative texts: Sequential texts that tell stories through the actions of characters, through a narrator's voice, or some combination of the two. This term is usually applied to works of fiction, although, of course, when people talk to one another they often tell stories about things they or others have done. Gossip often has a narrative, linear, sequential form characterized by some combination of elements in the "he said/she said/I said/we said/they said" formula.

Place: The setting where the events in a narrative text occur. Place is one of two major orientation devices used by authors (the other is time). Audiences learn to read the meanings of settings, and certain actions and activities, logically speaking, take place only in specific settings: Operations require hospitals, trials require courtrooms, and so on.

Plot: The way an author tells a story and arranges for events to occur. Plots involve series of actions that are connected to one another and that are resolved, ideally, in a logical and satisfying manner. Plots generally include conflict of some kind that generates interest, suspense, and other emotions in readers. Conflict can be external, between characters or between a character and some institution, for example, or it can be internal, in the mind of a character. If there is no conflict or opposition, there is no suspense to tie events together and make readers interested in the outcome of the story. Authors must make many choices in plotting; an infinite number of things can happen to people, and authors must choose particular ones to generate desired effects. According to Aristotle, in a well-constructed plot everything hangs together, and changing one thing will wreck the plot's unity and impact. It is also possible to imitate the stream of consciousness and to offer audiences random events from which they can construct some kinds of stories in their own minds.

Point of view: The vantage point from which the author creates a narrative. Bal (1985) prefers the term "focalization," because she believes most discussions of point of view are deficient and misleading. Most analyses of point of view deal with omniscient narrators, naive narrators, and so on. Bal notes: "All these typologies have proved more or less useful. They are all, however, unclear on one point. They do not make an explicit distinction between, on the one hand, the vision through which the elements are presented and, on the other, the identity of the voice that is verbalizing that vision. To put it more simply: they do not make a distinction between *those who see* and *those who speak:* Nevertheless, it is possible both in fiction and in reality, for one person to express the vision of another" (pp. 100-101). She prefers the term *focalization,* then, which she defines as "the relationship between the 'vision,' the agent that sees, and that which is seen" (p. 104). The most general questions we have to ask in thinking about point of view are (a) Who is telling the story—one person or a number of different people? and (b) How much does the storyteller know about what is going on in the minds of the various characters? For example, a story may be told by an omniscient author who moves in and out of the minds of various characters, by various characters taking turns relating events in the first or third person, or by one character (who may or may not be the main character or protagonist of the story) relating events in the first person.

Recognition or **Anagnorisis:** A character's sudden realization of his or her situation and what he or she can expect in the future. Recognition scenes are often found in tragedies, when the protagonist suddenly discovers or recognizes the full importance of what has happened and gets an inkling of what is to come.

Resolution or **Denouement:** The way things turn out in a story after the climax. The resolution should fit the nature and scope of the action that has occurred before it. A resolution that involves a minor character who has not been shown to have adequate motivation (the butler did it) or the use of some other unexpected or improbable event brought in at the last moment is considered to weaken a narrative. The term *deus ex machina* (literally, "a god from the machine") is often applied to such resolutions; it comes from an ancient practice of ending stage plays by having a player in the role of a god wrap everything up after being lowered onto the stage by a crane.

Stock characters: Characters who are recognizable as particular types, stereotyped figures whose natures are easily recognized by readers. Stock characters enable authors to take shortcuts and give readers a sense of the behavior to be expected of these characters and the motivation for their actions.

Story: The various events that occur in a narrative. The story is not identical to the text; a given story can be told in a number of different texts. For example, in films, many stories have been told several times; there are two versions of *King Kong* for instance, and three of *A Star Is Born,* not to mention reworkings of the same stories made under different titles. The basic stories are the same (or very similar), but they are told somewhat differently each time, using different actors and actresses, emphasizing different themes, and so on.

Subplot: A secondary plot involving minor characters and their relationships.

Summary: A recapitulation by the narrator or one of the characters of important events that have transpired so far. Summaries are useful to remind readers what has happened in a story up to a certain point and to focus attention on certain events that authors want their readers to pay attention to or keep in mind.

Symbolism: The use of objects, events, or actions to stand in for things outside themselves. Thus in *The Maltese Falcon,* the statuette has symbolic significance, representing the villain's greed and obsessiveness and, by implication, the greed of a number of others who are willing to lie, cheat, and kill to get their hands on it. The bird turns out, ironically, to be made of lead, and thus also symbolizes the futility of much human action and the genius individuals have for acting in self-destructive ways. A symbol is something that conventional knowledge tells us stands for something else; thus we have to be taught what symbols mean. The word *symbol* comes from the Greek *symballein,* which means "to put together." Thus a symbol brings two things together—for example, an object and an act by a character that has some higher meaning. Critics often distinguish between allegory and symbolism, using the latter term for something that has a fixed, transcendental significance and the former for one whose meaning becomes evident as the action progresses.

Text: Generally, any work that can be "read"—whether a film, a television program, a comic strip, a print advertisement, a television commercial, or something else. Bal (1985) defines a text as "a finite, structured whole composed of language signs" (i.e., words) (p. 5). Deciding what constitutes a text can sometimes be problematic. Consider, for example, a soap opera that has been broadcast on television for 30 years. When critics deal with this soap opera as text, do they have to deal with all 30 years (impossible, obviously) or can they focus on some segment of it or even one day's installment?

Theme: A message a narrative conveys about life and human relationships. Consider, for example, *Murder on the Orient Express*—the story is about the ritual murder of a man on a train by a group of people, but its themes include the importance of justice being done and the value of compassion.

Time: Along with place, one of the basic orientation devices found in texts. It is often important for readers to know the time period in which a text's action takes place because this can play a role in the way they interpret the meanings of various events. Westerns, for example, take place at the end of the nineteenth century, when the American legal system had not been established throughout U.S. territory, and science fiction usually takes place in the future, when various technological marvels, such as spaceships, will be (or so it is thought) commonplace.

Tone: The style of writing and the attitude or feeling displayed by the author toward the readers and what occurs in the text. An author can adopt any tone he or she chooses in creating a text—playful, serious, ironic, solemn, or something else. The use of the term *tone* in reference to texts was made popular by the work of I. A. Richards.

Voice: The persona of the author displayed in the text. Voice may be said to be almost synonymous with tone, for the voice of the author is the major element in tone. One could say that it is voice that creates tone. If an author's voice is, for instance, insouciant and smart-alecky, this tells readers how they should feel about the events taking place in the story and also reveals the author's attitudes about these events.

A Final Note

In this brief glossary, I have listed and briefly described a number of the most important concepts used by critics in dealing with narrative texts. There is much more to literature, of course, than narrative texts—even though, as I pointed out earlier, much of our television viewing involves narratives, as does much of our reading. Even nonfiction genres such as historical books, science books, biographies and autobiographies, and reference books of all kinds do, in fact, have a narrative structure—because, I would suggest, it is narratives that most closely approximate our lives, our way of functioning in the world and making sense of it. If "all the world's a stage," as Shakespeare tells us it is, then it is stories that we see on that stage; in many cases, the stories that interest us most are our own stories, but we also find other stories interesting and useful because we are diverted from our cares and worries by them, often can learn from them, and derive some comfort from their resolutions (which we do not find in our lives).

dream: A psychic phenomenon occurring during sleep in which thoughts, images, emotions, etc. present themselves to the dreamer, usually with a definite sense of reality. Dreams are not random psychic productions, for they fulfill a vital purpose in the mental economy. They safeguard sleep; they foster a solution in phantasy of needs and conflicts too dangerous for solution in reality; they provide an outlet for the discharge of instinctual tension; they allow a working through of destructive and traumatic experiences which defy the coping capacities of the waking state. Dreaming is a universal psychic function, typical of the human mind. It is one of the vehicles by which impulses from the unconscious reach the level of consciousness. . . . Because sleep includes a shutting out of sensory receptors and progressive cortical inhibition, the dream itself works in the manner of the primitive mental apparatus. Visual images tend to replace words, thinking becomes archaic and distorted, and there is a tendency toward a universal language.

Leland E. Hinsie and Robert Jean Campbell, *Psychiatric Dictionary* (1970)

5

Dreams

A Freudian Perspective

A s we pass through the life cycle, we are exposed to a number of different kinds of narratives in a variety of media—lullabies our parents sing to us (or play to us on records or on CD-ROMs), nursery rhymes, children's stories (often beautifully illustrated), fairy tales, comic strips and comic books, television dramas, adolescent novels and adult novels, films, and games on video and CD-ROMs.

In the 1930s and 1940s, when I was growing up, radio broadcast many action-adventure genre narratives, such as *The Lone Ranger, The Green Hornet, Jack Armstrong, The Shadow, Counterspy,* and *The FBI in Peace and War.* Children growing up in those decades had, in radio, a "theater of the mind" that made use of their imaginations. This was in contrast to what we get today on television, which one wit has described as the "theater of the mindless."

In the chapters that follow, which are devoted to some of the more important kinds of narratives, I will discuss fairy tales, comics, novels, television narratives, commercials, and films. In each chapter I will say something about the nature of each kind of narrative and then, when possible, analyze a significant text. These chapters deal, in sequence, with the kinds of narratives we encounter as we move from infancy to adolescence to adulthood. The last four items on the list are all generally experienced about the same time, though the kinds of novels we read and the television programs and films we like tend to become more complicated and sophisticated as we get older, moving through adolescence and into adulthood. This chapter is devoted to our first narratives—dreams.

Freud's Theory of Dreams as Wish Fulfillment

Dreams are, quite likely, the first narratives we experience, and they are a continuing source of what might be described as the narrative "experience." The average person typically dreams every night for approximately 2 hours. Each of us is, then, the creator of a number of narrative texts every night, as well as the hero or heroine (and in some cases the victim) in these narratives. Sigmund Freud, whose book *The Interpretation of Dreams* (1900/1965) is the source of this discussion, asserts that dreams take the form of images that we stitch together into narratives when we recall or recount them.

According to Freud, dreams, in essence, function as wish fulfillment: "*When the work of interpretation has been completed, we perceive that a dream is the fulfillment of a wish*" (p. 154). Freud's notion that dreams are essentially wish fulfillment is, I should point out, a highly controversial thesis—but that matter is not essential to our concerns here.

Freud suggests that our minds forget nothing, that we remember all of our experiences, even those that do not register on our minds. Memory plays an important part in dreams, and some dreams are about experiences we had in our earliest years that are lodged deep in the unconscious realms of our psyches. Freud (1900/1965) writes:

> The way in which the memory behaves in dreams is undoubtedly of the greatest importance for any theory of memory in general. It teaches us that "nothing which we have once mentally possessed can be entirely lost" (Scholz, 1893: 59); or, as Delboeuf (1885, 15) puts it "even the most

insignificant impression leaves an unalterable trace, which is indefinitely capable of revival." (p. 15)

This notion is worth keeping in mind, because it might offer some insights about why we respond to narrative texts as we do. It is possible that these texts, as well as dreams, speak to readers' buried and repressed memories.

There is a problem that arises, however. We have to be careful, when we dream, that the wish fulfillment in which we are indulging does not alert our dream censors, agents for all practical purposes of our conscience and moral sensibilities. We have to disguise our wishes, which often are of a sexual nature, and outsmart the dream censor—a situation that Freud suggests is analogous to a political writer who has "disagreeable truths to tell those in authority." As Freud explains it, dreams assume the shapes they do in individuals because of the operation of two psychic forces. One force constructs the wish that is expressed by the dream, and the other force exercises censorship on this dream-wish. As a result of this censorship, there is a distortion in the expression of this wish in the dream. This distorted expression of the wish is of major importance, for it explains why our dreams (and symbolic phenomena in narratives) take the forms they do and have the impacts they have.

What is important, for the moment, is that we understand that dreams are composed of images that we experience as narratives when we dream and that we put these discrete images into a narrative structure when we remember them and recount them. These discrete images are, however, distorted and use various tricks to evade dream censorship—in the same manner that filmmakers used to use certain devices to evade film censorship.

Freud on Decoding Dreams

Freud suggests that there are essentially two popular methods of interpreting dreams. The first, he says,

considers the content of the dream as a whole and seeks to replace it by another content which is intelligible and in certain respects analogous to the original one. This is "*symbolic*" dream-interpretation; and it inevitably breaks down when faced by dreams which are not merely unintelligible but also confused. . . .

Most of the artificial dreams constructed by imaginative writers are designed for symbolic interpretation of this sort: they reproduce the writer's thoughts under a disguise which is regarded as harmonizing with the recognized characteristics of dreams. (p. 129)

Freud does not believe that this is the best method of interpreting dreams. His comments about artificial dreams, however, can be extended to cover narrative texts and to suggest that these texts are, in interesting ways, connected to the dreams and imaginations of creative writers.

Freud then discusses the second popular method of dream interpretation, which, he says, can be described as a kind of decoding that treats dreams as a form of cryptography, in which every sign in a dream can be seen as representing another sign whose meaning is known in accordance with a fixed set of interpretations (p. 13). He mentions dream books that claim to tell readers what given symbols in dreams mean, without consideration of who is doing the dreaming. He mentions a modification of this method that can be found in the work of an ancient Greek, Artemidoris of Daldis:

This method takes into account not only the content of the dream but also the character of the dreamer; so that the same dream-element will have a different meaning for a rich man, a married man, a bachelor or a merchant. The essence of the decoding procedure, however, lies in the fact that the work of interpretation is not brought to bear on the dreams as a whole but on each portion of the dream's content independently, as though the dream were a geological conglomerate in which each fragment of rock required a separate assessment. (pp. 130-131)

He even quotes, in a footnote, a writer who suggests that we make sense of dreams by interpreting them in terms of their opposites.

Although Freud is talking about interpreting dreams, it is not difficult to see the relevance of his theories for narrative texts in general. His use of the word *decoding* anticipated the use of the word by contemporary critics. Dreams, Freud says, really do have meaning, and there is a scientific means of interpreting this meaning; we might not agree with the use of the word *scientific* in connection with decoding or analyzing narrative texts, but most critics believe that texts can be interpreted and that some methods of interpretation are better than others.

Elements in Dreams

There are a number of processes that go on during dreaming, and these have been described in a succinct manner by Erich Fromm in his book *The Forgotten Language* (1957). Fromm explains that dreams require interpretation that must be keyed to the dreamer's life and experiences. Fromm discusses Freud's ideas about the various elements in dreams:

> The true dream, which is the expression of our hidden desires, Freud calls the "latent dream." The distorted version of the dream as we remember it is the "manifest dream." The main mechanisms through which the dream-work translates the latent into the manifest dream are condensation, displacement and secondary elaboration. By condensation Freud refers to the fact that the manifest dream is much shorter than the latent dream. It leaves out a number of elements of the latent dream, combines fragments of various elements and condenses them into one new element in the manifest dream. . . . By displacement Freud refers to the fact that an element of the latent dream, and often a very important one, is

expressed by a remote element in the manifest dream and usually one
which appears to be quite unimportant. (pp. 69-70)

We fill in the gaps in dreams, repairing inconsistencies through a process
called "secondary elaboration."

What makes interpreting dreams difficult, however, is that in dreams
elements frequently stand for their opposites, and dreams themselves,
we must recall, are not coherent narratives but series of disconnected
images that we unify in our minds. The process of condensation, it has
been suggested, is similar to the linguistic process of using metaphor
(analogy) and the process of displacement is similar to that of using
metonymy (association).

Symbols in Dreams

Freud discusses the nature of symbolism in *The Interpretation of
Dreams*. He explains that symbolism is found in places other than dreams
and is characteristic of the process of unconscious ideation. He adds that
symbolism is also found in folklore, popular myths, legends, proverbial
wisdom, linguistic idioms, and jokes to a greater extent than in dreams.
Analyzing symbols, he continues, is very complicated and problematic
because of the way dreams disguise latent thoughts. But it is possible to
point out that some symbols are "habitually employed to express the
same thing" (p. 387), even though we must be careful to focus attention
on the individual dreaming and the individual's dream.

Although we cannot say that a symbol always means a particular
thing in a dream, certain symbols—by virtue of their similarity to geni-
talia, in shape or in function—tend to have specific meanings. Thus
Freud (1900/1965) writes:

> All elongated objects, such as sticks, tree-trunks and umbrellas (the
> opening of these last being comparable to an erection) may stand for the
> male organ . . . as well as all long, sharp weapons, such as knives, daggers
> and pikes. . . . Boxes, cases, chests, cupboards and ovens represent the
> uterus . . . and also hollow objects, ships and vessels of all kinds. . . .
> Rooms in dreams are usually women. . . . Steps, ladders or staircases, or,
> as the case may be, walking up or down them, are representations of the
> sexual act. (pp. 389-390)

Many people find far-fetched—if not ridiculous—Freud's suggestions that, in dreams, objects have symbolic sexual dimensions and certain kinds of behavior are symbolic representations of the sexual act. Freud, of course, would defend himself by saying that people with these views are repressing this knowledge, refusing to recognize material that they find disturbing for one reason or another.

A Freudian Analysis of a Dream:
A Case Study

In an article titled "The Occurrence in Dreams of Material From Fairy Tales" (1963), Freud offers a case study in the analysis of dreams. He recounts the dream of one of his patients, a young married woman who had sex with her husband (who had been away for several months) a few days before she had her dream. This is the woman's dream:

> She was in a room that was entirely brown. A little door led to the top of a steep staircase, and up this staircase there came into the room a curious manikin—small, with white hair, a bald top to his head and a red nose. He danced round the room in front of her, carried on in the funniest way, and then went down the staircase again. He was dressed in a grey garment, through which his whole figure was visible. (A correction was made subsequently: *He was wearing a long black coat and grey trousers.*)

Freud makes a number of points in his analysis of this dream. First, the story of Rumpelstiltskin came to the woman's mind, for in the story Rumpelstiltskin had danced around in the same strange way as the man in the dream and had, in so doing, betrayed his name to the queen. As a result of doing this he lost his claim to the queen's first child and, in a fit of anger, tore himself in two. Second, the woman had been very angry with her husband on the day before she had the dream and had exclaimed, "I could tear him in two." Third, the brown room was, on the most immediate level, the woman's double bed, but on a deeper level, Freud suggests, it had a sexual meaning: "The room, at this level, was the vagina. (The room was in her—this was reversed in the dream.) The little man who made grimaces and behaved so funnily was the penis. The narrow door and the steep stairs confirmed the view that the situation was a representation of coitus" (p. 61). Fourth, the woman was able to interpret the transparent gray garment as a condom. The woman had been worried about conceiving and this, Freud suggests, may have played a role in generating the dream. Fifth, the black coat and gray trousers refer to the way the woman liked to see her husband; she wanted to convince him to dress well, instead of wearing his usual clothes. And finally, Rumpelstiltskin was connected to the day's residue in the woman's psyche by an antithetic relation and offered insights into the infantile stratum of dreams. As Freud (1963) writes:

> The droll little fellow, whose very name is unknown, whose secret is so eagerly canvassed, who can perform such extraordinary tricks—in the fairy tale he turns straw into gold—the fury against him, or rather against his possessor, who is envied for possessing him (the penis envy felt by girls)—all of these are elements whose relations to the foundations of the patient's neurosis can, as I have said, barely be touched upon in this paper. The short-hair of the manikin in the dream was no doubt also connected with the subject of castration. (pp. 61-62)

Because we do not know much about Freud's patient, we cannot assess how accurately he represents her and her problems, but his analysis of her dream is an excellent example of the kind of interpretation that Freudian critics make not only of dreams, but also of fairy tales (as we will see in the discussion of Bruno Bettelheim's work in Chapter 6) and other kinds of texts as well.

I find, generally speaking, that my students tend to dismiss Freud's arguments out of hand as absurd. Although they usually consider his notions to be ridiculous, they are able to apply Freud's concepts to television programs and films and other texts with considerable facility. The question I pose to them is one we might consider: Why, if Freud is ridiculous, is it so easy to find phallic symbols, vaginal symbols, and all kinds of other phenomena from Freud's theories in texts?

Dreams and Fairy Tales

By dealing with a fairy tale that was part of a woman's dream, Freud also makes an important point. Not only are dreams narratives, but these highly personal narratives are connected in interesting ways to fairy tales

TABLE 5.1 Differences Between Dreams and Fairy Tales

Dreams	Fairy Tales
wish fulfillment disguised	wish fulfillment expressed
individual's problems the focus	general problems the focus
pressures unresolved	pressures resolved
uncontrolled	shaped over history
personal, private	general, public
fugitive	long-lasting

and other kinds of narratives to which people are exposed. There has been some attention paid in recent years, for example, to the ways films and television programs have "invaded," so to speak, people's dreams. Literary theorists talk about the notion of "intertextuality," by which they mean that texts often draw upon, imitate, and are otherwise connected to (whether consciously or unconsciously) other texts. This theory may help us understand why some of our dreams take the forms they do.

And Freud reminds us that in dreams, and other kinds of narratives as well, there is always a hidden symbolic (generally sexual) significance to much of what characters say and do, and to the objects they use in their everyday lives. This sets the stage for the discussion of another kind of narrative, the fairy tale. Bruno Bettelheim, whose book *The Uses of Enchantment* (1976) is considered to be one of the most important studies of this genre, explains how dreams function (p. 54). He suggests that fairy tales contain dreamlike aspects that are akin to what we find in the dreams of adolescents and adults, but not of children.

Although an adult's dreams may seem incomprehensible, when these dreams are analyzed all their details eventually make sense and enable the dreamer to understand what has preoccupied his or her unconscious mind. Thus we can gain significantly better understanding of ourselves by comprehending aspects of our mental lives that have escaped our notice, been distorted, or have not been recognized before.

Dreams are connected to inner pressures that individuals face that they have not relieved, and dreams, Bettelheim suggests, don't succeed in relieving them. Fairy tales, on the other hand, deal with general pressures that all people face and suggest acceptable solutions. Generally speaking, wish fulfillment is disguised in dreams, whereas it is much more openly expressed in fairy tales. Table 5.1 lists some of the differences in the functions of dreams and fairy tales. We can see that there are considerable differences between dreams and fairy tales. It is to fairy tales we now turn, to explore the narrative elements and psychological significance of this important genre.

Fairy tales are the bedtime stories of the collective consciousness. They persist in the cultural memory because they interpret crises of the human condition that are common to all of us. They are shared wish fulfillments, abstract dreams that resolve conflicts and give meaning to experience. Philosophers of myth have sketched the genealogy of fairy tales, tracing most of them back to primitive *rites de passage* and initiation rituals. In some way, most of them celebrate the metaphoric death of the old inadequate self as it is about to be reborn on a higher plane of existence. Like Charon's boat, they grant us passage to a world where the mortal and the eternal, the sacred and the secular, meet; where the past and the future are divined; where good and evil clash, but where goodness, truth and beauty are destined to victory. Fairy tales are thus primarily metaphors of the human personality, of the individual psyche's struggle to be free of fear and compulsion.

The omnipresence of myths and fairy tales in so many aspects of culture—speech, idioms, poetry, music, dance, painting, sculpture, drama, fiction, film—suggests that these stories describe and narrate the structures of a collective as well as individual experience.

Madonna Kolbenschlag, *Kiss Sleeping Beauty Good-Bye* (1981, p. 2)

6

Fairy Tales

Fairy tales are, Bruno Bettelheim (1976) suggests, the most important kinds of stories (that is, narratives) we are exposed to as children. This is because, for reasons that will be explained shortly, they are vital to the psychic development of young children. They are also, I will suggest, a protonarrative, or *ur-narrative*, from which other popular genre narratives have evolved.

In the analysis that follows I draw primarily upon Bruno Bettelheim's *The Uses of Enchantment: The Meaning and Importance of Fairy Tales* (1976) and Max Lüthi's *The Fairytale as Art Form and Portrait of Man* (1984), though I use material from other sources as well. Luthi tends to focus upon stylistic and aesthetic matters and Bettelheim on the psychological meanings of fairy tales, but both authors consider fairy tales as a genre and have important things to say about them.

Defining the Fairy Tale

I have already discussed fairy tales to some degree in Chapter 2, in which I presented a number of the fundamental elements that Propp (1928/1968) has found in typical fairy tales, though he limits his analysis

83

to certain Russian folktales. In this section I will briefly discuss some of
the defining elements of fairy tales, to expand and enhance the reader's
understanding of the nature of these stories.

First, *fairy tales generally begin "Once upon a time,"* or open in some
other way that serves the same function—that of setting the narrative off
from the present, from the everyday world of the reader, listener, or teller.
This use of the past, Lüthi (1984) suggests,

> has a specific narrative function, not just in the sense that it fictionalizes,
> as in the theory of Kate Hamburger, but also in that it clearly indicates
> that henceforth a closed and thus easily surveyable train of events is to
> be described. . . . The opening lines "once upon a time" . . . establish
> distance. They create distance from the present and, along with it, from
> reality, and offer an invitation to enter another world, a world past, thus
> one that does not exist. (p. 40)

So this kind of opening has an important narrative function. It situates
the story in the past and suggests that it takes place in a different world,
one far removed from that of the teller, listener, or reader.

Second, *fairy tales generally end with the hero or heroine triumphing and
the assurance that "they lived happily ever after."* This also generates distance
and gives closure to the story. Rumanian folklorist Mihai Pop has sug-

gested that the openings of fairy tales lead children from reality to the unreal and that their closings bring them back from the unreal into the real. Bettelheim asserts that such endings also reinforce the notion that the child who is listening to the story, like the hero of the story, can overcome obstacles and succeed in finding happiness in life.

Third, *fairy tales have a basic bipolar structure*. Lüthi (1984) delineates this structure, noting that in fairy tales we find extremes and polarities characterized by "clarity, compactness, and exactitude" (p. 54):

> The polarity minus/plus is the framework and the basis of the structure of the fairy tale, in its entirety just as in individual details. . . . A lack (or a villainy which causes a lack) and its liquidation provide, according to Propp, the basic structural pattern of the fairytale. Alan Dundes has coined the abbreviation L-LL: Lack/Lack Liquidated for this pattern. (p. 54)

Thus we see that there is an elemental simplicity to the fairy tale based on bipolar opposition. One might add, keeping in mind Propp's notions about the kinds of heroes and heroines we find in fairy tales, that there is also a secondary polarity: villainy/defeat of villain. Lüthi continues with some typical situations found in fairy tales:

> Examples of situations of lack are, according to Propp: The hero has no bride, so he sets out to seek one; the king is ailing and in order to restore his health, medicinal water or a magic bird must be fetched. . . . Examples of villainies are the kidnapping of the czar's daughter; the doing away with of a magical helper by the antagonist. . . . One sees that lack (e.g. poverty) can result in villainy (the setting out of the children); a villainy (e.g. robbery) for its part leads automatically to a lack. . . . The Lack/Remedy is in fact the basic pattern of the fairytale and, moreover, of countless stories and things that occur in life in general. (pp. 54-55)

This pattern is connected to our everyday lives, in which we often experience the equivalent of fairy tale "lacks" (or, as I have suggested, suffer from the actions of "villains") and do what we can to remedy these situations. Connected to this lack/remedy structure is the general matter of happiness/disturbance/happiness restored and other secondary polarities—prohibition/violation, need/help, task/fulfillment, kidnap/rescue, and so on. Many of these are polarities that I have sketched out in Table 2.3, in which I took Propp's functions and turned them into sets of oppositions.

Bettelheim (1976) explains how the use of such polarities helps young children deal with their problems. He explains that fairy tales characteristically suggest existential dilemmas to children quickly and pointedly. They enable children to recognize problems in their most essential form, whereas more complex stories may confuse them. Fairy tales also simplify all situations. Their figures are drawn clearly, and most details, unless they are very important, are eliminated. Characters in fairy tales, therefore, are typical rather than unique. Thus the simplicity of the fairy tale plot assists young children, who lack the ability to understand ambivalence and ambiguity, both to understand the nature of the problem the tale deals with and to identify with the heroes and heroines of these tales.

Bettelheim (1976) contrasts fairy tales with what we find in many modern children's stories that present a sanitized picture of reality:

> Contrary to what takes place in many modern children's stories, in fairy tales evil is as omnipresent as virtue. In practically every fairy tale good and evil are given body in the form of some figures and their actions, as good and evil are omnipresent in life, and the propensities for both are present in every man. It is this duality which poses the moral problem, and requires the struggle to solve it. (pp. 8-9)

Bettelheim also notes that the polarization we find in fairy tales reflects the polarization that dominates the mind of the young child, who cannot understand ambiguities at this stage of development. I would add that adults also polarize, recalling Saussure's (1966) notion about the way concepts are interpreted and Jakobson's (1985) suggestion that the mind finds meaning by setting up bipolar oppositions.

Fourth, *fairy tales center on the actions of heroes and heroines.* All the other figures are of secondary importance and are used to provide complications, to set the action in motion, to help the hero or heroine accomplish some task, and so on. The heroes and heroines tend to be young, weak, common individuals, and often we only know their first names (as is the case with Jack in "Jack and the Beanstalk"). The characters are typical and not unique, and this, I would suggest, allows children to identify with them more easily.

Fifth, *in fairy tales good and evil are omnipresent and the difference between them is sharply drawn.* Characters are either good or evil. This is because, as Bettelheim points out, young children have not reached the level of psychological development necessary for them to deal with ambiguities and subtle distinctions. When young children are exposed to texts that have moral ambiguities at too early an age, as is the case when they watch certain television programs (soap operas, for example), they may experience psychological trauma that can affect their ability to relate to others in their adult years.

The above discussion gives a highly generalized picture of the fairy tale. Not all fairy tales take identical form, but the elements listed are all typically found in fairy tales. They are highly formulaic stories passed down through the ages, and they tend to have conventional beginnings and endings; they are simply drawn, and do not go into detail as a rule; and they have young, common, ordinary heroes and heroines who are sharply delineated from the various villainous figures who battle with them. These heroes and heroines generally either confront some villain or strive to take care of some lack, and do so with the aid of helpers and magic objects.

Fairy tales were originally oral in nature, one result of which is that there are many different versions of particular stories, even though they are now available in written form. With fairy tales it is the story that is important, not the text. Different texts may vary in minor details, but as long as the basic elements of the story are intact, the fairy tale will work its magic.

Fairy Tales, Myths, and Fables

At this point I would like to differentiate fairy tales from genres that are often linked to them: myths and fables. Considerable differences can be identified between myths and fairy tales and between fables and fairy tales. Myths are generally defined as "sacred stories." They involve matters such as the creation of the world and the activities of various gods and demigods.

Drawing on Bettelheim's ideas in his chapter "Fairy Tale Versus Myth," Table 6.1 suggests some differences between these two genres.

TABLE 6.1 Comparison of Myths and Fairy Tales

Fairy Tales	Myths
indirect	direct, didactic
ordinary heroes, heroines	gods and demigods, superhuman characters
typical, generalized characters	particularized heroes and heroines
simple presentation	majestic presentation
no demands made on readers	demands made on readers
the typical	the unique
happy endings	tragic endings (often)
optimistic	pessimistic
ego integration depicted	superego dominant

We can see that there are considerable differences between fairy tales and myths. Myths play an important part in our psychological development, but they are useful to people when they are older and can deal with the psychological complexities of these stories. As Bettelheim suggests at the end of his chapter on myths and fairy tales, myths project ideal personalities who act on the basis of their superego demands. Fairy tales, on the other hand, depict an ego integration that makes possible the proper satisfaction of id desires. This explains why myths tend to be pessimistic and fairy tales are generally optimistic.

Bettelheim alludes to Freud's notion that the human psyche has three components: the id, ego, and superego. This is known as Freud's "structural hypothesis." The three components may be described in simplified form as follows:

- *Id:* desire
- *Ego:* perceiving reality and adapting to it
- *Superego:* guilt

The ego functions as a mediating force between id forces and superego forces. If either id or superego overwhelms the ego and becomes too strong, neurosis and psychological problems occur.

Bettelheim also distinguishes between fables and fairy tales. Fables, he says, "tell by means of words, actions, or events—fabulous though these may be—what one ought to do" (p. 27). The kind of moralism found in fables is not found in fairy tales. Bettelheim quotes Samuel Johnson's definition of a fable:

> A fable seems to be, in its genuine state, a narrative in which beings irrational, and sometimes inanimate, are, for the purpose of moral instruction, feigned to act and speak with human interests and passions. (p. 42)

The problem with fables, Bettelheim asserts, is that they are too explicit, too overtly moralistic, and leave nothing to the imagination of the child. He points out that if a child happens, by chance, to identify with the grasshopper in the fable of the ant and the grasshopper, there is no hope left—only doom awaits the child who has made this identification.

With this overview of the general nature of fairy tales in mind, I would like to turn now to the way fairy tales function, to the way they work their magic with children. I will focus here on the ideas of Bruno Bettelheim and others concerning the psychoanalytic significance of these tales.

The Way Fairy Tales Function: A Psychoanalytic Perspective

Bruno Bettelheim, it should be stated, tends to be a somewhat doctrinaire Freudian; that is, he uses Freud's concepts without significant modifications to analyze the behavior of the characters in fairy tales and to interpret the way fairy tales function. In the introduction to *The Uses of Enchantment*, he explains how fairy tales help young children with their development:

> Through the centuries (if not millennia) during which, in their retelling, fairy tales became ever more refined, they came to convey at the same time overt and covert meanings—came to speak simultaneously to all levels of the human personality, communicating in a manner which reaches the uneducated mind of the child as well as that of the sophisticated adult. Applying the psychoanalytic model of the human personality, fairy tales carry important messages to the conscious, preconscious, and the unconscious mind, on whatever level each is functioning at the time. By dealing with universal human problems, particularly those

which occupy the child's mind, these stories speak to his budding ego
and encourage its development, while at the same time relieving preconscious and unconscious pressures. As the stories unfold, they give conscious credence and body to id pressures and show ways to satisfy these
that are in line with ego and superego requirements. (pp. 5-6)

We have to recognize, Bettelheim asserts, that young children experience
all kinds of psychological pressures as they grow up. They need stories
that they can understand to help them deal with these pressures (although they are unaware of what is happening, of course).

Bettelheim mentions some of the difficulties young children experience as they grow up—narcissistic disappointments, sibling rivalries,
childhood dependencies that have to be relinquished, and oedipal dilemmas—and discusses some of the things they must do, such as gain a
sense of self-worth, a sense of moral obligation, and a feeling of selfhood.
Fairy tales help children by enabling them to fit their unconscious
conflicts onto conscious fantasies and suggest ways children can structure their fantasies to help give better direction to their lives. Children
cannot usually articulate the problems and pressures they face, but they
experience them with great intensity—as any parent who must deal with
sibling rivalry can acknowledge.

Bettelheim offers an analogy that is useful here. He mentions the use
in Hindu medicine of fairy tales to help disturbed people deal with their
problems, and explains:

> In a fairy tale, internal processes are externalized and become compre-
> hensible as represented by the figures of the story and its events. This is
> the reason why in traditional Hindu medicine a fairy tale giving form to
> his particular problem was offered to a psychically disoriented person,
> for his meditation. It was expected that through contemplating the story
> the disturbed person would be led to visualize both the nature of the
> impasse from which he suffered, and the possibility of its resolution.
> (p. 25)

The fairy tale offered didn't necessarily have anything to do with the
external life of the disoriented person, but had to do with his internal
conflicts. By contemplating the story, the person found his own solution
to his problems.

It is quite conceivable that many of the narrative texts people watch on television (or experience in other media, such as print, radio, and film) function the same way. That is, these texts speak to certain needs people have, and thus the choices people make among texts are often connected to deeper things than they imagine, such as unconscious conflicts and problems. At any given moment in an evening, a viewer has many choices among different television programs. Why is it he or she chooses certain programs? Is it possible that many of these programs are, in essence, fairy tales that have been modified and camouflaged one way or another?

The fairy tales that children love may be unreal, Bettelheim points out, but they are not untrue. That is, the characters are made up and exist in made-up worlds, but the kinds of things they experience are all too human and strike a responsive chord in children—and in adults as well. But the listener must make sense of the tale—thus Bettelheim cautions that adults should never explain fairy tales to children.

Bettelheim says that fairy tales begin exactly where a child is from an emotional standpoint and show the child where he or she has to go and how to go there. Fairy tales do this by implication, using fantasy material that children can make sense of and relate to their problems. Children can draw on these stories as they need to, because the stories use images that make it easy for them to understand what is essential and important for them to understand. A child may become anxious when hearing a particular story, but once he or she becomes acquainted with fairy tales in general, the troubling aspects of these stories tend to disappear and the reassuring aspects become more dominant. The original anxiety the child feels turns into pleasure based on facing and mastering that anxiety.

This matter of generating anxiety and then relieving it, one way or another, is at the heart of most narratives; it also is a source of pleasure in other experiences, such as riding roller coasters and other scary rides in amusement parks. Anxiety is generated and then relieved, leading to feelings of mastery.

Children learn some very important ideas from fairy tales, Bettelheim tells us. They learn that they need help to gain their ends, which means they must submit to some of the demands of their helpers; they learn that they must leave home to find the magic kingdom they seek (and the prince or princess of their dreams), and that doing so involves taking risks and enduring trials and ordeals. But ultimately, children learn from these stories that they will triumph, and this gives them the psychological support they need at their stage in the developmental process.

In the first half of *The Uses of Enchantment*, Bettelheim deals with psychoanalytic processes and the way they relate to fairy tales, discussing a number of them briefly. In the second half of the book he offers extended analyses of a number of classic tales, such as "Hansel and Gretel," "Little Red Riding Hood," "Jack and the Beanstalk," "Snow White," and "Cinderella." His discussion of Cinderella is the longest of the analyses, almost 40 pages long. I would urge anyone interested in the relation of fairy tales to psychological processes or in psychoanalytic criticism of texts to read this material. As an example of how Bettelheim uses psychoanalytic theory to explicate fairy tales, I will analyze his brief, but very perceptive, discussion of *A Thousand and One Nights* (also known as *The Arabian Nights* or *1,001 Arabian Nights*) from the first part of the book.

A Synopsis of
A Thousand and One Nights

Let me first offer a brief synopsis of *A Thousand and One Nights*, a collection of stories from Persia and India. The story of Sheherezade is a frame story that introduces the collection (and ends it, after the last story has been told).

A king named Shahryar has become very angry and terribly disillusioned with women because he has discovered that his wife has been unfaithful to him (with black slaves) and that the same thing has happened to his brother, King Shahzeman. In addition, a powerful jinni has also been betrayed by a woman he thought he had locked up carefully.

Shahryar finds out about his wife's betrayal from his brother, who has grown weak because he is suffering from an internal wound—the notion that nobody can love him. The same idea, we are led to believe, afflicts Shahryar. He decides to give his life over to lust and sensual pursuits, but vows also that he will not allow a woman to betray him again, so every evening he sleeps with a virgin and then has her killed the following morning. Finally, no young virgins are left in the kingdom except Sheherezade, the daughter of the grand vizier. The grand vizier doesn't want Sheherezade to go to King Shahryar, but she insists on doing so in order to become his "means of deliverance."

Sheherezade tells her younger sister, Dunayazad, to come to the king's bedroom after Sheherezade and the king have had sex and ask Sheherezade for one of her delightful stories. Sheherezade then tells a different story every night, but doesn't finish it, so the king doesn't have her killed in the morning because he wants to hear how the story ends. She ends one story and begins another each evening for 1,001 days. At the end of the 1,001 days, Dunayazad is replaced during the storytelling by the king's and Sheherezade's little son. Sheherezade declares her love for the king, and he declares his love for her and his trust in her, and they live happily ever after.

A Psychoanalytic Interpretation
of *A Thousand and One Nights*

Any text has a number of possible interpretations, depending on the point of view, disciplinary identification, political beliefs, and so on of the person making the interpretation. Even if one adopts a psychoanalytic perspective, there are many different schools of psychology, so one can even expect differences among psychoanalytic interpreters. This discussion follows Bettelheim's essentially Freudian analysis.

Bettelheim starts off by pointing out that the story involves a man and woman who meet during a crisis in each of their lives: The king hates women and is disgusted with life; the woman faces death but is determined to save the king from himself and to save herself as well. She does these two things by telling the king many, many fairy tales. She needs to do this, Bettelheim suggests, because people's psychological problems are very complex and difficult to solve. They require a number of tales (each of which has something to contribute to the healing process) to generate the catharsis that is needed. It takes almost three years of the continued telling of fairy tales to help the king escape from his depression and become cured. He has to listen, attentively, to fairy tales for a thousand nights in order to reintegrate his personality, which had become completely disintegrated.

We can describe the king as a person who is completely dominated by the id elements in his personality because his ego, as a result of severe disappointments in his life, has lost its ability to restrain his id. Sheherezade, symbolically speaking, is an ego figure, but one whose superego is so strong that she willingly risks her life to save the king. Thus we have two characters who both need each other and help balance one another. The king is an id figure dissociated from his ego and superego, and Sheherezade is a superego-dominated ego figure separated too much from her id.

Sheherezade cannot deliver the king from his depression until she changes herself and achieves psychological integration. As Bettelheim points out, it takes a person whose ego can draw on the positive energies of his or her id for positive purposes to use that ego to control the murderous impulses in the id. Sheherezade's love for King Shahryar inspires her storytelling. Psychoanalytically speaking, her superego (save women from being killed by the king) and id (her love for the king) both work together to save the king and, in doing so, become an integrated personality.

So Sheherezade gains a great deal from the experience herself; she weakens her superego, which has been dominating her ego, and gains energy from connecting to her id. The king's personality becomes integrated due to Sheherezade's love and the fact that he is now a father. His murderous hatred has been changed to love.

Bettelheim then generalizes from this story to assert that it teaches us, among other things, that everyone has to go through many different developmental crises, centering on the problems of personality integration and control of oedipal conflicts. This latter phenomenon involves finding a way to separate from our parents and the power they have over us and the power we give them due to our anxieties and dependency needs.

The reason fairy tales are so important for children, Bettelheim argues, is that these tales not only entertain children but also help them find ways to deal with the psychological pressures from which they suffer and to gain an element of ego integration.

An Analogy With Psychotherapy

I should point out also that the story of Sheherezade calls to mind, in certain ways, what Freud called "the talking cure." In this process, a person suffering from neurotic problems "talks" with a therapist (some-times over a long span of time) and, as a result of a variety of things that happen, is helped or becomes cured.

One of the purposes of psychoanalysis is, according to Freud, to free people from domination by their ids and help them nourish their egos. "Where there is id let there be ego" is the famous phrase he used. (Those wishing to find out more about psychoanalytic theory and practice would do well to consult Charles Brenner's *An Elementary Textbook of Psychoanalysis*, 1974, one of the best introductions to this complicated subject.) It took 1,001 stories to cure the king, and it sometimes takes a considerable number of sessions to help some individuals deal with their problems.

Brenner (1974) suggests that fairy tales are usually the first kind of stories that interest children because these tales deal with childhood instinctual fantasies. He also argues that, when one probes their deepest meanings, significant narratives are all ultimately connected to oedipal themes. He notes, "For a literary work to have a strong, or, even more, a lasting appeal, its plot must arouse and gratify some important aspect of the *unconscious oedipal wishes of the members of its audience*" (p. 235; emphasis added). The connections are not obvious, and people are not generally aware of the role oedipal issues play in their lives, but the reason works "resonate" in us, Brenner asserts, is that the connection is made, at a level below that of our consciousness.

In a sense, one can say there is one "hidden" or "real" (what Jungians would call an "archetypal") story that underlies all the other stories we tell ourselves or tell others—the story, disguised and camouflaged in many different ways, of our battle to resolve what may be described broadly as our oedipal conflicts. So all stories are, in reality, one story— the same old story—a fight sometimes for love and sometimes for glory, and sometimes for both.

The Fairy Tale as Ur-tale

Let me offer a hypothesis here. I suggest that the fairy tale, our first significant narrative (according to Brenner and Bettelheim), is what might be called an ur-narrative—the basic story from which other kinds of stories draw sustenance. That is, the various elements found in fairy tales, when spun off and elaborated, give rise to most of the other popular culture genres, such as detective stories, science fiction stories, horror stories, and romances. Consider the following abbreviated story, which is typical of the fairy-tale genre:

> Once upon a time, long, long ago, a strange creature—half man and half bird—flew into a kingdom and made off with the daughter of the king. The creature planned to eat the princess when he got hungry. The king offered his daughter's hand to whomever could rescue her. A young boy set off in search of the princess. In the course of his wandering, he saved a bird that was caught in a trap and helped an old man who had fallen into a ditch. The man, who was a wizard, gave the boy a magic sword and a magic carpet that would fly through the air. The bird was a magic bird that could find anyone or anything. It went flying all over the kingdom and found the princess, then flew back and told the young man where she was imprisoned. The young man jumped on his magic carpet and sped to the castle of the creature. It was getting hungry and preparing to eat the poor princess. The boy battled the creature and cut its head off with his magic sword. He then flew back to the king's palace with the princess. The king was so happy to see his daughter again that he ordered a big celebration. The boy and the princess got married and lived happily ever after.

In this simple little story, we have the seeds of a number of different popular culture genres:

- *Horror:* the strange creature
- *Detective:* setting out to find the kidnapped princess
- *Science fiction:* magic carpet analogue of rocket ship
- *Action-adventure:* fought with the creature
- *Romance:* married the princess

All of these genres take elements from fairy tales and develop those elements (and related narrative features) to a considerable degree. It is not too much of a step, if you think about it, from a creature that eats princesses to a dragon that breathes fire, to a Dracula or a Frankenstein's monster.

From fairy tales, the most important kind of narratives we encounter in childhood (from a psychological point of view), we move to comic strips—one of the earliest kinds of print narratives to which we are exposed and probably the first form of print narrative we are able to read and understand on our own. It is also one of the longest lasting, given that it is not unusual for particular comic strips to continue to appear for 40 years or more—or even longer in some cases, when the original artist is replaced.

Narration or storytelling is also a main function of the comics. They are meant to be read, as opposed to traditional narrative art meant to viewed and interpreted. While they have never competed with the classics, they have seriously altered popular reading habits by attracting readers away from pulp magazines, dime novels, and cheap tabloids (only detective and science fiction have withstood the competition and survived). The total work of some cartoonists constitutes something like a novel on the pattern of Balzac's human comedy or Faulkner's Yoknapatwpha County cycle. *Little Orphan Annie* follows the picaresque pattern of *Adventures of Huckleberry Finn,* and *Gasoline Alley* anatomizes an entire midwestern community much in the tradition of Sherwood Anderson's *Winesburg, Ohio* or Sinclair Lewis' *Main Street* (especially with the recent emphasis by Dick Moores and his successor Jim Scancarelli on the provincial grotesque).

It has been suggested that the comics are closest to drama in that both rely on the dramatic conventions of character, dialogue, scene, gesture, compressed time, and stage devices, but probably the motion picture is closer. Will Eisner, distinguished for his visual innovations in comic art, has stated that "comics are movies on paper."

M. Thomas Inge, Comics as Culture (1990, pp. xix-xx)

7

The Comics

The comic strip is an art form that is found in various kinds of print media—newspapers, magazines, books—as well as in electronic media and animated films. In this chapter I will discuss some of the narrative elements found in print (more specifically newspaper) versions of comic strips, which is where we have found them for the past 100 years, and in comic books, which have been popular since the 1930s.

Defining the Comic Strip

Let me begin by quoting a definition from M. Thomas Inge's *Comics as Culture* (1990) that sets the stage for my analysis: "The comic strip may be defined as an open-ended dramatic narrative about a recurring set of characters, told in a series of drawings, often including dialogue in balloons and a narrative text, and published serially in newspapers" (p. xi). Note that Inge uses the word *narrative* twice in his definition, indicating the significance of this aspect of comic strips.

I will expand somewhat on Inge's definition here, and will discuss the three dominant aspects of comics: their narrative structure, their pictorial content, and their use of dialogue and other linguistic elements.

99

Let me point out that there is a difference between comics and cartoons. Cartoons, as a rule, do not have continuing characters; they also generally have only one frame, and the dialogue is not in balloons but is usually found in a caption beneath the cartoon. *The Far Side*, for example, is not a comic strip but a cartoon; it has certain types of characters, but it doesn't have the same characters appearing regularly.

The Narrative Structure of Comics

Generally speaking, comics are presented in strip form. The English translation of the French term for comics is "designed bands." That is, they contain a number of frames that show characters interacting with one another—talking, fighting, doing various things. These characters, as mentioned above, continue on from episode to episode. The frames generally include dialogue, usually in balloons, attached one way or another to speakers, so we know who is saying what to whom. In addition, sometimes at the bottom of a frame or in separate frames, we may find information designed to help with continuity—the equivalent of a narrator's voice.

There are two narrative structures found in newspaper comics: serial strips, in which the action carries over for a number of different episodes, and what might be called "gag" strips, in which each day is a complete episode. Many of the strips in the 1930s and 1940s, such as *Li'l Abner, Dick Tracy,* and *Little Orphan Annie,* were serial in nature, and story lines often went on for a month or two before being resolved. Most of the newer strips are gag strips, with new gags each day. Some newer strips also combine humorous situations on a daily basis with background serial stories.

Readers of comics confront a sequence of discrete frames. (This isn't always the case; some comic strip artists break out of the frames at times, but usually comics are frame bound.) Each frame contains a drawing of characters and, generally speaking, dialogue. The readers of comics must unify these frames in their imaginations and create a coherent story from them—much the same way people who go to films see a sequence of images projected at high speed that gives the illusion of action. And much the same way, as I have pointed out in the discussion of dreams, dreamers take a number of images and create a story from them when they remember their dreams and recount them—a process Freud calls "secondary elaboration."

The limitations of the comic strip as an art form require comic strip artists to condense action and to create strongly delineated characters, both good and evil, with whom readers can easily identify. One of the reasons comic strips are so popular is that their narrative structure tends to be very elemental and easy to grasp. But readers must bring a good deal of knowledge to reading comics: They must know how to decode various signs, such as scalloped balloons indicating thoughts and lines around arms and legs indicating movement, and they must understand something about the thought processes of the characters, which are not always spelled out, and their emotions.

The characters in humorous strips tend to be comic types—gluttons, fools, henpecked husbands, lovesick women, naughty boys, pets who may be philosophical but are interested essentially in food—with whom we can all identify. Thus the comics provide a narrative structure that is relatively simple and easy to follow. Because of the power of the pictorial image linked to language, comics have proven to be a very flexible art form and are used in everything from advertisements to instruction manuals. (There are even books in comic strip format devoted to Freud and to Marx.)

In recent years, comic strip artists have adapted the comic strip to longer narrative forms, and we now have what are sometimes described as pictorial novels—novels that use the comic strip format to tell their tales. An example of this is Art Spiegelman's *Maus* (1986), a work that deals with a very serious subject—the Holocaust. There are many others as well.

The Pictorial Content of Comics

When we read comics, not only do we unify the frames in our imaginations and read the words the characters speak (and the narrators provide for us here and there), we also scrutinize the drawings. We do this to see what the characters are doing and to determine, to the extent we can, how they feel about what they say. We try to "read" the expressions on their faces to get a better understanding of what is motivating them and what they are like.

So the pictorial element of comics is very important; we follow some characters for years, sometimes for decades. Comics can be described as an iterative art form, one in which our familiarity with the characters over the years gives us a sense of considerable familiarity with them (with good reason, given that many of us grow up with them) and thus an increased pleasure in following their adventures.

The graphic style of the artist also is often significant. Thus the strong blacks and whites in *Dick Tracy* and the grotesques created by Chester Gould generate a sense of morbidity and menace that permeated the strip. On the other hand, Herriman's fanciful drawings in *Krazy Kat* enhance the sense of whimsy and absurdity found in this remarkable comic—considered by many scholars to be the greatest American comic strip ever created.

A number of filmmakers have studied the kinds of shots found in the frames in comics to learn something about how to shoot films. Comic strip artists generally vary their frames considerably, to keep them interesting to readers and to avoid the boredom of repeating the same frame (shot) over and over. Comic strip artists need dialogue to indicate what characters are thinking and to tell something about what is going on, and they need drawings to create characters with whom their readers can identify, characters their readers find interesting, amusing, or exciting.

Dialogue in the Comics

Earlier comics, in the 1930s and 1940s, tended to have much more dialogue than do contemporary ones—especially gag strips. And some of this dialogue was quite remarkable. Let me quote from one of my favorite examples—an episode in *Li'l Abner* in which Marryin' Sam describes what he provides in an eight-dollar wedding ceremony:

> Fust—Ah strips t' th' waist, an' rassles th' four biggest guests!! Next—a fast demon-stray-shun o' how t' cheat yore friends at cards!!—follyed by four snappy jokes—guaranteed t' embarrass man or beast—an'—then after ah dances a jig wif a pig, Ah yanks out two o' mah teeth, an' presents 'em t' th' bride and groom—as mementos o' th' occasion!!—then—Ah really gits goin!!—Ah offers t' remove any weddin' guest's appendix, wif mah bare hands—free!! Then yo' spread-eagles me, fastens mah arms an' laigs t' four wild jackasses—an' bam!!—you fires a gun!! While they tears me t' pieces—Ah puffawms th' weddin' ceremony!! (quoted in Berger, 1994, p. 58)

To my mind, this passage is a brilliant piece of writing; I use it to show the possibilities for writing in the comics. Not every comic strip has the superb dialogue found in *Li'l Abner* or *Krazy Kat*, of course—but my point is that there is nothing about comic strips, as an art form, to prevent a comic strip artist from writing good dialogue. We also find superb dialogue in many contemporary strips, such as *Calvin and Hobbes* and *Doonesbury,* and a number of nonmainstream and underground comics as well.

The Complex Matter of "Reading" the Comics:
The Katzenjammer Kids

Reading the comics is much more complicated than it might seem. In part this is because comics are what Marshall McLuhan (1965) describes as a "cool" and not a "hot" medium (I would use the term *art form* instead of medium). Cool media, according to McLuhan, have relatively little information and, as a result, generate a good deal of participation. He contrasts, for example, a photograph with a cartoon or comic strip; photographs generally carry an enormous amount of information, whereas comic strips do not.

Comics require their readers to interpret every sign (every facial expression, action, thought, use of language, and so on) available and to bring to the comics an understanding of human behavior and motivation. Readers fill in the outline provided by the comic strip, so to speak. Let me illustrate this point by using a comic strip that has no dialogue in it but that we are nevertheless able to understand; in effect, the reader creates imaginary dialogue to explain the action.

The episode I will analyze is from Rudolph Dirks's *The Katzenjammer Kids*; this particular strip was first published February 2, 1930. The strip deals with the continual battles waged by the Kids, twins Hans and Fritz, with three adult figures—Mama (often shown spanking the Kids for stealing pies or wielding a rolling pin as a weapon), the Captain (a shipwrecked sailor who functions as a father figure), and the Inspector (a school administrator).

In this episode, the Captain and the Inspector steal a cake that is cooling in Mama's kitchen. Mama sees footprints and follows them; she stops following the footprints when she comes across the Kids, who are innocently fishing, and, thinking they have stolen the cake, gives them a spanking. The Captain and the Inspector see this but don't do anything, and when Mama has gone back home, they bring the cake to a clearing and start eating it. The Kids see them and decide to get revenge. They create a contraption to simulate footprints and steal a pie that is cooling in the kitchen. They make the footprints lead to the Captain and the Inspector. Mama follows the footprints and dispenses justice with her rolling pin. Then the Kids, carrying their pie and their footprint contraption, walk by the Captain and the Inspector.

There are numerous graphic devices used in the strip to help us understand what is going on. In the first frame, we see a long ribbon of smell leading from the cake to the Inspector's nose. That is, we are shown that he is smelling a cake. In the next frame we see the Captain and the Inspector peering into the kitchen. Heat lines are emanating from a cake

The Katzenjammer Kids

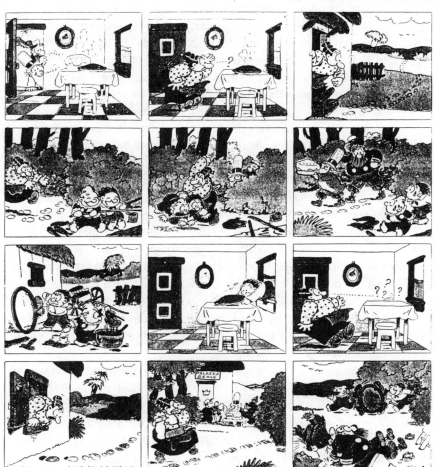

SOURCE: Used by permission from King Features, *The Katzenjammer Kids*.

and pie that are cooling on a table, and "SNIFF!" is shown underneath the noses of the Captain and the Inspector. We do not actually see them take the cake, but in the third frame, Mama looks at the table and notices the cake is gone. There is a dotted line leading to her eyes and a big question mark signifying that she wonders what has happened to the cake. We are led to assume that the Captain and the Inspector have taken the cake. Our familiarity with the characters of the strip over the years gives us good reason to make this assumption—though even if we don't know the characters well, the logic of the narrative suggests, very strongly, that they have taken the cake.

In the next frame Mama sees footprints and, putting two and two together, she concludes that these footprints were made by the people who stole the cake. If you look at the footprints carefully, you can see that they were made by one person; that is, we don't have two sets of footprints. Dirks is merely indicating, in a general way, that there are footprints, and is not trying to be realistic. Mama follows the footprints and in the next frame comes across Hans and Fritz, who are innocently fishing. Assuming that they stole the cake, and not following the foot-prints further, she gives them a good spanking—while the Captain and the Inspector look on, hidden in the bushes. The expressions on the faces of the Kids show they are suffering greatly as they are spanked. The following frame shows the Kids crying as the Captain and the Inspector walk past them, carrying the cake. The Captain lifts his hat, to acknow-ledge that he has seen them. In the next frame, the Kids, with angry expressions on their faces, figure out how to get revenge. They take a hoop and put shoes on it to make a device that generates a line of footprints; then they steal the pie.

When Mama comes into the kitchen she is really surprised (as we can see from her body language) and we see four question marks, indicating that she wonders what has happened to the pie. She looks out the window and sees the footprints. Armed with a rolling pin, she follows the footprints, comes across the Captain, the Inspector, and a friend eating the cake. We have here only the suggestion of footprints, for there is only a line of single footprints, which is not what you get when a person walks. In the last frame, Hans and Fritz, carrying their pie, walk by the adults who have been soundly thrashed by Mama. The Kids are shown smiling—having gotten revenge and, in addition, having a nice pie for themselves to eat.

Because there is no dialogue in this strip, we are forced to provide our own interpretations of what is going on—though we are helped by the various graphic devices Dirks uses to carry the story forward: the smell line, the heat lines rising from the newly baked cake and pie, the question marks, the facial expressions, and so on. There is not a great deal of variety in the shots; most of the frames are either medium shots or long shots, but they depict a variety of scenes, so the strip is not visually boring.

When you add dialogue to a comic strip, you can develop character more completely and create much more involved stories. But as the episode I have just analyzed demonstrates, visual aspects of comics play an important part in the scheme of things, and it is possible to generate an interesting story with only drawings and visual cues.

On the Status of Comics in the Scheme of Things

Let me conclude by dealing again with the status of comics relative to other art forms—such as novels, plays, and paintings. As I pointed out earlier, we frequently make a distinction between popular arts and popular culture and their opposites, the so-called elite arts, or what I sometimes describe as "unpopular culture." The elite arts generally include such things as operas, ballets, classical music of all kinds, serious poetry, and nongenre novels. The popular arts include rock music (and other kinds of popular music, such as country-western), comics, genre fiction (romance novels, detective novels, science fiction novels), and so on.

In a *Calvin and Hobbes* strip that first ran on July 20, 1993, Bill Watterson deals brilliantly with this very subject. In the first frame of the strip, Calvin looks at a painting.

CALVIN: A painting. Moving, spiritually enriching. Sublime. "High" art!

In the next frame, Calvin and Hobbes look at a page of comics.

CALVIN: The comic strip. Vapid. Juvenile. Commercial. "Low" art.

Calvin and Hobbes then look at an art book and find a work of pop art—a painting of a comic strip.

CALVIN: A painting of a comic-strip panel. Sophisticated irony. Philosophically challenging. "High" art.

In the last frame we find Calvin doing a drawing. Hobbes asks a question:

HOBBES: Suppose I draw a cartoon of a painting of a comic strip?

Calvin replies:

CALVIN: Sophomoric. Intellectually sterile. "Low" art.

Here we have what might be described as a philosophical analysis, in a comic strip, of the nature of comic strips and their relation to other art forms. (In other strips Calvin suggests that he's a postmodernist because his mother won't let him be a deconstructionist.) The phenomenon of pop art raises a difficult question for those who wish to classify art forms into low and high or popular and elite arts. Works of pop art have sold for more than $2 million in recent art auctions—does that mean that a frame from a comic strip, magnified and painted in oils, is in significant ways different from the comic strip frame itself? Or is there something wrong with our notion that there are important differences between popular and elite art forms?

The comic strip is an important and ubiquitous narrative art form, and some really marvelous comic strips are published all over the world. An Italian publishing house, Garzanti, put out a big collection of comics a number of years ago titled *I Primi Eroi,* which can be translated loosely as *Our First Heroes.* The characters in comics may not be our first heroes and heroines (I would give that position to the characters in fairy tales), but they are among our first heroes and heroines and they are ones we grow up with, reading about them daily, and following them for many years of our lives. Some comic strip characters, through merchandise spin-offs (dolls, sheets, towels, blankets, plates), actually have a presence in our lives that is much stronger than the one they have in the newspapers. These characters not only amuse us, but in many cases they have become part of our lives.

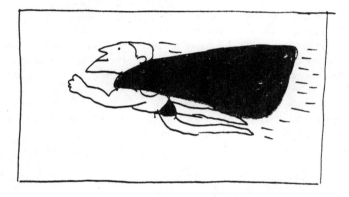

Nichols' McDonald's spots possess the most accelerated time sense of any on television. "Quick Cuts" [the title of one of Dan Nichols' commercials] contains more cuts than can be counted: after repeated viewing the author had to slow down the tape to count 65 different scenes in 60 seconds. A seven-second segment of this spot contains fourteen separate scenes, or two per second. Incredible as it may seem, it *is* possible for the viewer to perceive these different scenes even though they go by faster than they can be counted.

The effect on the viewer is a sense of extreme urgency and of the present tense: the action is thrust into the immediate present because it is rendered as more alive and exciting than even the most engaging real-life experience. Nichols taps the "live" associations of television in this way more insistently than any other director. Because of the sense of urgency and presentness which the spots communicate, the viewer actually experiences the exciting lifestyle Nichols depicts rather than passively observing events which occur to someone else. . . . More than promoting a particular product, these spots advertise an appealing way of life associated with the restaurant, causing the viewer to turn to the product for gratification.

Bruce Kurtz, *Spots: The Popular Art of
American Television Commercials* (1977, p. 94)

8

The Macintosh "1984"
Television Commercial
A Study in Television Narrativity

Television is a medium through which we can view many kinds of programs or genres made available in many ways—through broadcast signals, cable, satellite, and, with the use of a VCR, prerecorded videocassettes. So, from a technical standpoint, we are really talking about video images when we use the term *television* loosely. Nowadays many films are also shot in video, and some theorists argue that eventually all films will be shot this way.

The Image on Television

When we say that an ordinary person in the United States watches almost 4 hours of television each day (which means that by age 65 the average American has spent 9 years sitting in front of a television set), we don't mean that the person is interested in the mosaic of dots found on the screen; rather, we refer to the person's involvement with the programs available on this medium—or its competitors. As Martin Esslin (1982) has suggested, much of the television programming we watch is composed of narratives, which can be loosely defined as fictional stories about invented characters, as I have noted previously.

In film theory, it is possible to identify the smallest unit of measure quite easily. It is the single frame. But what is the smallest unit of measure in television (and I use the term loosely here—the way most people do)? There are no frames in video, only mosaics of dots endlessly re-forming to generate images. Here is how Marshall McLuhan (1965) has described the matter:

> With TV, the viewer is the screen. He is bombarded with light impulses that Joyce called the "Charge of the Light Brigade" that imbues his "soulskin with subconscious inklings." The TV image is visually low in data. The TV image is not a still shot. It is not a photo in any sense, but a ceaselessly forming contour of things limned by the scanning finger. . . . The TV image offers some three million dots per second to the receiver. From these he accepts only a few dozen each instant, from which to make an image. (p. 313)

From the millions of dots generated in a video picture, we select a number of them and form them into an image. There is also an audio component to watching television; not only do we watch but we listen at the same time, and though sometimes we can make sense of things we see without the audio, we can usually do so only in very general terms.

McLuhan has argued that "the medium is the message," by which he means that the programming on television is not the most important aspect of this medium. Television, according to McLuhan, alters our sense of ratios or patterns of perceptions, and thus has a more general impact than we might imagine.

A Brief Primer on Television (Video) Aesthetics

The question arises: If there are no frames to function as the primary unit in television, what, if anything, has this function? My answer to that would be the *shot*. Vladimir Propp (1928/1968) argues that the most elemental unit in the fairy tale is what he calls a function—an act of a character relative to the story itself. I would transpose this notion to the video medium and say that the most elementary unit in video is the shot, the manner in which a camera follows some course of action.

For our purposes, a shot can be defined as a segment of action in a televised narrative that exists between cuts, dissolves, or other editorial decisions that end one shot and lead to a new one. Some television shots, of course, are longer than others, so we don't have units that are all equal, the way we do in film. But taking shots as our fundamental unit does give us something to work with.

Each shot and the editing procedures used to make transitions between shots are kinds of cues that tell us something. When the camera moves in, we are being told, by the visual equivalent of a narrator, "Pay attention—something important is going on, some detail is going to be made known to you." A shot in which the camera looks up toward a person makes that person seem large and powerful—just the opposite of what happens in a shot that looks down on a person. A z-axis shot extends vertically from the screen to viewer, instead of going across the screen, horizontally. Because television screens are relatively small, directors have more scope for action on the z-axis, moving toward viewers or away from them.

Table 8.1 offers a brief list of some of the basic kinds of shots and camera work and what each signifies. We all have to learn something about what shots mean if we are to make sense of what we see on television; we do this learning informally, of course, by watching television programs. Most people who watch television, although they are able to read the meanings of various shots and camera work, are not familiar with the terminology used by people in the industry and don't give any thought to the technical aspects of the medium.

The size of the television image also confers a certain status on it; television is a very intimate medium, which we observe in the privacy of our living rooms. As Esslin (1982) notes:

> Television is the most voyeuristic of all communication media, not only because it provides more material in an unending stream of images and in the form most universally acceptable to the total population, but also because it is the most intimate of the dramatic media. In the theater, the actors are relatively remote from the audience, and the dramatic occasion

TABLE 8.1 Meanings of Shots and Camera Work

	Definition	*Meaning*
Shot		
close-up	small part of body	intimacy
extreme close-up	very small part of body	inspection
medium shot	most of body	personal relations
full shot	all of body	social relations
long shot	setting and characters	context, scope
z-axis	vertical action toward viewer	involvement
wipe	image wiped off screen	imposed end
dissolve	image dissolves into next one	weaker ending
Camera work		
pan down	camera looks down on X	power of viewer
pan up	camera looks up at X	weakness of viewer
dolly in	camera moves in	observation
fade in	image appears on screen	beginning
fade out	image disappears from screen	ending
cut	switch from one image to next	excitement

SOURCE: Based on ideas developed in Berger (1991).

is public. In the cinema, also a public occasion gathering a large audience into a single room, the actors are nearer to the spectators than in the theater, but in close-ups they are larger than life. Television is seen at close range and in a more private context. The close-up of the television performer is on a scale that most nearly approximates direct human contact. (pp. 30-32)

We often have the illusion, when we watch television—which is generally described as a "close-up medium"—of actually being *with* other people. That is why people often have parasocial relationships with television performers, that is, they feel (or, more precisely, they have the illusion) that they "know them" intimately. That may also explain why lonely people often find television comforting; relying on close-ups as much as it does, the medium provides people who watch it with a spurious kind of companionship, a (visually speaking) virtual community of sorts. But this pseudocompanionship is not satisfying in the way real companionship is, because we are social animals, not parasocial animals. Thus, as the law of diminishing returns starts to operate, people who use television this way (for a spurious sense of companionship) must watch more and more television to get the "benefits" they used to get with less television watching.

The Macintosh "1984" Commercial

The Macintosh "1984" commercial, directed by Ridley Scott, director of such films as *Alien* and *Blade Runner,* was shown only once on television (during the 1984 Super Bowl) as a commercial. It is one of the most celebrated commercials of recent times, and was made (I was told by an advertising executive from Chiat/Day) at a cost of around $500,000. It cost approximately $800,000 to air it.

I have chosen this text for analysis here both because of its aesthetic values and sociocultural significance and because the storyboard for the commercial is available. We can analyze the "1984" text in terms of the 10 shots shown on the storyboard, which I will discuss in some detail following a brief synopsis.

The commercial begins with the date "1984" appearing on the screen. It cuts to an extreme long shot of figures marching; we can vaguely perceive them as they march in a long tunnel that joins gigantic structures. The next cut leads to a long shot of the figures marching; their heads are shaven and they wear ill-fitting, dull uniforms. Their faces are expressionless. The commercial then cuts to a close-up of the heavy boots of the marchers. Next, there is a quick cut to a brief shot of a blonde woman wearing a white jersey and red shorts, running. The camera cuts back to the dull, expressionless figures in the uniforms (Skinheads Scott recruited for the commercial). In the next shot, the blonde woman is being pursued by a group of helmeted troopers. The commercial then cuts to an extreme long shot of the inmates of the institution sitting in a huge room, gazing at an enormous television screen. A figure wearing glasses is shown on the screen speaking to the inmates, who sit gazing at the screen in a trancelike state. The man on the screen talks to them about their being free and so on. Suddenly the blonde woman, who is carrying a sledgehammer, runs into the room. She hurls the sledgehammer at the screen, which explodes. The inmates sit through all this with dazzled and stupefied expressions on their faces, staring at the screen. A

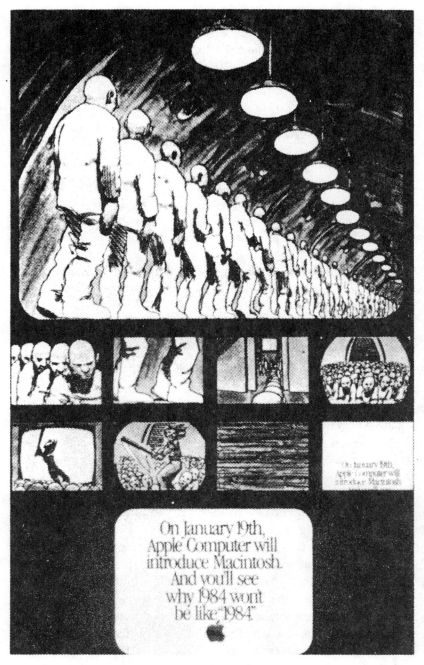

SOURCE: Used by permission from Apple Computer, Inc.

message from Apple then appears, announcing the introduction of the Macintosh computer.

The storyboard for "1984" has 10 images, which I will describe in turn below.

1. A long shot of the marchers, who form a seemingly endless line. This shot provides us with an overview and establishes the context in which the microdrama will be played out. The marching figures are all deperson-alized. In the commercial, this is exaggerated by placing the figures in a gigantic building of some kind, with long corridors snaking here and there. The size of the building in the commercial makes the marchers appear even less human and more insignificant than they are in the storyboard.

2. A close-up of the marchers' heads. This close-up of the marchers, all of whom have shaved heads, further intensifies their image as dehuman-ized prisoners in some kind of total institution. In the commercial, the images of the marchers, with their shaved heads, suggest extreme deper-sonalization.

3. An extreme close-up of the marchers' legs and boots. This image adds to the previous ones and suggests the extent to which the inmates of the institution are controlled, marching in unison. The extreme close-up of their heavy boots is an example of synecdoche (a part representing a whole) and is meant to add to the impression that these are people who are completely dominated. This shot also has intertextual meaning, because it calls to mind shots used by Sergei Eisenstein in *Battleship Potemkin* and other shots of figures wearing boots and marching in unison, though some of these shots have been of armies, storm troopers, and so on. All of the ideas and associations called to mind by this extreme close-up are negative and disturbing.

4. An extreme long shot of the inmates filing into an auditorium. This shot introduces visual variety into the commercial and offers a bit of narrative information: the inmates, whom we saw marching earlier, are shown filing into a large auditorium dominated by a gigantic television screen.

Television, we are led to infer, plays an important role in this dehuman-
ized total society.

5. *An extreme long shot of the inmates in a large auditorium.* With this
shot, we now have the inmates seated and we see them all watching the
screen that was shown in the previous shot. There is a huge number of
inmates. We can see, in retrospect, that the first five shots have all been
of the inmates as they marched toward and into the auditorium.

6. *A medium shot of a woman swinging an object.* Here we are introduced
to the heroine of this drama, an attractive blonde woman who shows that
not everyone is enslaved, that there are elements of resistance in this
institution or society. In the background we see a huge television screen
that is the object of attention of the members of the audience. In the
commercial, we see the blonde woman, her breasts heaving, racing
ahead of a pack of burly guards who are pursuing her.

7. *A second medium shot, from the opposite angle, of the woman swinging
an object.* In the storyboard, the object looks like a bat or a piece of wood;
this is replaced in the commercial by a much more symbolic sledgehammer. We also see a huge screen (with a gigantic head on it mumbling
gobbledygook) that is the object of her attack.

8. *A shattered screen.* This is one of the most significant images in the
commercial. The woman has thrown her sledgehammer at the screen and
shattered it. In so doing, we are led to believe, she has inflicted a mortal
wound on the organization that enslaves the inmates by, so it is suggested, controlling their minds. In the commercial, the skinheads sit
transfixed by the speaker on the huge television screen. After the screen
has been shattered, they have astonished looks on their faces.

9. *The beginning of the Apple Macintosh announcement starts scrolling.*
We see the Apple Macintosh announcement beginning to appear.

10. *The full Apple Macintosh announcement is on screen.* The announcement reads: "On January 19th Apple Computer will introduce
Macintosh. And you'll see why 1984 won't be like '1984.' " The commer-

cial plays off of comparisons between the year 1984 and George Orwell's imagined future of that year in his dystopian novel *1984*.

Symbology and Mythic Aspects
of the Commercial

The Apple logo, an apple with a bite out of it, also has an intertextual (in this case, mythological) significance, in that it alludes to Adam and Eve in the Garden of Eden. The bite can be understood to represent Adam's bite, which gave him knowledge of good and evil and led to humankind's being banished from Paradise. With this in mind, it is possible to see still other intertextual connections.

The blonde woman with her sledgehammer is a kind of David figure who hurls a missile at a giant, Goliath-like brainwasher (the huge head on the television screen in the auditorium) and kills him. She also can be seen as an Eve figure who leads humans to a knowledge of good and evil, though she is functioning in a dystopian institution, just the opposite of the Garden of Eden.

The shots of the inmates and the expressions on their faces all suggest a prison, some kind of gigantic total institution (or total society) where a mass of brainwashed, zombielike figures are held captive. These figures contrast with the color, vitality, and sexuality of the blonde woman, who runs into the auditorium (in a z-axis shot) ahead of the police, who are chasing her. They cannot prevent her from destroying the Big Brother image, and when she does so, we are led to think, she shatters the control this figure and the organization he represents have over the inmates.

It is possible to read this text as a kind of parable, with the total institution enslaving the alienated proles as representing, in an exaggerated way, IBM, the "Big Blue," a company known for being somewhat authoritarian—making its workers dress conservatively and so on (this has apparently changed somewhat in recent years). Another reading would suggest that IBM is the Big Brother figure and that the American public is represented by the inmates. (Still a third reading suggests itself also: The power of the televised image over the American public will be shattered when a computer that any ordinary person can run—the Macintosh—is made available to the general public.)

In any case, it is Apple computer, represented by the beautiful blonde woman, who will save everyone from indoctrination and, in the more general context of the battle between Apple Macintosh and MS-DOS personal computers, from the complications and brain-numbing problems involved in using MS-DOS personal computers. The commercial works not by heralding the qualities of the Macintosh but by the use of aversion—suggesting through its use of images what IBM is like and, by association, what it is like using IBM (and IBM clone) personal computers.

The images the commercial encourages us to carry in our minds are of Apple computers as a beautiful blonde woman (who is also courageous and wants to save us from indoctrination) and of IBM as the bespectacled bureaucrat and his stupefied skinhead slave laborers.

Neutralizing the Power
of Television Narratives

In *Spots: The Popular Art of American Television Commercials*, published in 1977, when people weren't watching as much television as they are now, Bruce Kurtz calculated that "on average, each American sees 156 spots a day, or 1092 spots a week. One hour and eighteen minutes of the average American's daily television viewing consists of television spots, or about nine hours and six minutes a week" (p. 7). These figures are probably inaccurate now, because we watch more television now than we did in the 1970s. And many of the commercials aired today are only 10 or 15 seconds long, instead of the 30 seconds that was standard then.

This means that we are exposed to an incredible number of commercial microdramas, in addition to the other narratives we watch that contain these microdramas, in a typical day or week. If, as I have suggested earlier in this book, narratives play an important role in shaping our sense of who we are, in giving us ideas about what roles to play, and in giving us notions of how to behave when we deal with members of the opposite sex (and others), then we must develop methods of countering this indoctrination.

I believe we need to teach media criticism to our children in the public schools, starting in the early grades. We must find ways of countering the negative effects of television narratives of all kinds on our children and adolescents, and on adults as well. We may be more like the zombies in the "1984" Macintosh commercial than we imagine, and we need someone to help us break out of the trances we fall into when we turn on our television sets and stare at them for 4 hours each day (and there are addicts who spend considerably more time watching television).

Television in the United States is, I would suggest, like an invading fungus in a tree—you don't see anything from the outside, but the fungus slowly kills the tree. (There's nothing in the medium that makes it that way; rather, the economic arrangements, I would suggest, have led to the debasement of the medium.) Television is devastating our culture and corrupting our political life. Many would argue that television, more than any other medium (though the record industry might be a close second), is having a very negative influence on our children—exposing them to mind-numbing violence and excessive sexual excitement.

If we cannot figure out how to counter television's influence on our children, our institutions, and our society in general and somehow control it, there is no telling what its effects will be in the future. We may find, as we recall the "1984" Macintosh commercial, that we have become prisoners in a total institution or total society of our own making.

Peter Brooks briefly points to the fact that narrative seems to change in cultural importance at different moments of history and within different spheres of culture and consumption. Right now we seem to be in an age seeking beyond narrative, especially in areas of high culture. In popular fiction narrative desire and narrative forms, however, have remained central up till now and still seem to occupy the center of visual fiction. The popular desire seems to resist outspoken tendencies towards postmodern deconstruction and "antinarrative forms of thought." And even though the advent of Modernism, according to Brooks, could be described as an "era of suspicion toward plot" and we presently enter an era of deconstruction of even some forms of popular narrative, classical narration and generic coding of narrative, especially in television fiction, still place us in "an age of narrative plots":

> Narrative is one of the ways in which we speak, one of the large categories in which we think . . . the product of our refusal to allow temporality to be meaningless, our stubborn insistence of making meaning in the world and in our lives.

Ib Bondebjerg, "Popular Fiction, Narrative and the Melodramatic Epic of American Television" (n.d., p. 36)

9

The Popular Culture Novel

There is a considerable amount of debate among scholars about what a novel is and isn't and, in addition, when the form of fiction we know as the novel started. I will use a commonly understood definition of the novel as my starting point.

Defining the Novel

A novel is typically defined as a fictional prose narrative of extended length that portrays characters and has a sequential organization of scenes and actions. We can expand upon this definition by consulting Thrall, Hibbard, and Holman's *A Handbook to Literature* (1960):

> The term *novel* is used in its broadest sense to designate any extended fictional prose narrative. In practice, however, its use is customarily restricted to narratives in which the representation of character occurs either in a static condition or in the process of development as the result of events or actions. (p. 318)

Thrall et al. note that the term comes from the Italian *novella*, "a short, compact, broadly realistic tale" that was popular in the middle ages. We use the term *novella* now to refer to a narrative that is longer than a short story but shorter than a novel. In very broad measure, short stories can be any length from a few to 50 pages, novellas anything from 50 to 100 pages or so, and novels anything longer. However, it is hard to put numerical limits on art forms; who is to say that a given work is really a long novella rather than a short novel?

Thrall et al. (1960) add some information about the formal characteristics of novels:

> The *novel* may concentrate upon character, almost to the exclusion of incident or PLOT. It may be merely a series of incidents strung together on a string, as the PICARESQUE NOVEL tends to be. It may be firmly plotted, with a structure as firm and sure as that of a TRAGEDY. . . . It may attempt to present the details of life with a scientist's detached and objective completeness, as in NATURALISM; or it may try by IMAGE and linguistic and syntactic modification to reproduce the unconscious flow of the emotions, as in the STREAM-OF-CONSCIOUSNESS NOVEL. It may be episodic, loose in structure, epic in proportions—what is called "panoramic"—or it may be as tightly knit as a well-made play, bringing its material forward in dramatic orderliness—what is called "scenic." (p. 319)

We see, then, that *novel* is an umbrella term; it is really a site for all kinds of different forms and styles of narratives that can have different aims and purposes.

At the core, however, for a work to be called a novel, it must have the fundamental features of a novel. First, it must be fictional—about invented characters and not real people, though invented characters can sometimes be tied to real people and real people sometimes appear in novels. Second, it must be in prose, not in poetry, though the style of some novels is very poetic and lyrical. Third, it must be extended—long enough to develop the characters in considerable detail and to have a number of different events take place and be resolved in a satisfying manner. The novel's resolution must deal with the complications in the story and should conclude in a manner that is logical and reasonable. The extended nature of novels helps to differentiate them from short stories and novellas.

There are differing opinions about when the novel form originated, but most critics agree that *Pamela; or, Virtue Rewarded,* written by Samuel Richardson in 1740, is the first work that we can describe as a real novel. Novels differ from histories, which are about the lives and doings of real people, and from epics, which are usually long poems about national figures with superhuman and divine characteristics.

A novel can be about anything; it isn't the subject that is important but what the writer does with the subject, including what kinds of characters the writer creates and what events he or she has these characters involved in. There are numerous stylistic possibilities open to the novelist, which is why some critics describe the novel as a supergenre. Michael Holquist (1981), in his preface to Mikhail Bakhtin's *The Dialogic Imagination,* discusses Bakhtin's notions about novels and how they relate to other genres:

> Other genres are constituted by a set of formal features for fixing language that pre-exist any specific utterance within the genre. Language, in other words, is assimilated to form. The novel by contrast seeks to shape its form to languages; it has a completely different relationship to languages from other genres since it constantly experiments with new shapes in order to display the variety and immediacy of speech diversity. It is thus best conceived either as a supergenre, whose power consists in its ability to engulf and ingest all other genres . . . together with other stylized but non-literary forms of language; or not a genre in any strict, traditional sense at all. (p. xxix)

Novels, in a sense, resist definition, because they are always changing and novelists are always testing the limits of what novels are and can be.

There is also a controversy among literary theorists as to whether the characters in the novel or their actions are basic. Do characters' actions "create" (so to speak) the characters or do the nature and personalities of the characters lead to the actions? From my point of view what is important is that a novel's characters are interesting and that they do interesting things; whether character or action is primary is not a particularly important matter.

The novel in popular culture often is formulaic in nature, and many such novels can be classified as being in specific genres. The postmodernists have argued that there are no significant differences between works of popular art and works of elite art, or between popular culture and elite culture in general. As far as novels are concerned, I think this argument generally makes sense—a poor "serious" novel is a poor work and a fine "genre" novel is a fine work. A question suggests itself here: Does a "genre" novel like Dashiell Hammett's *The Maltese Falcon* lose its genre identity when it achieves a certain level of literary excellence? I will leave this question unanswered, but I suggest that there are, in many cases, differences between the novel, as we commonly understand the term, and the popular culture "genre" novel. It is to the popular culture novel that I now turn.

Popular Culture Novels

The novels I classify as popular culture novels are works that have all the attributes of the novel but also can be classified according to their genres—something one can't really do with a traditional novel. In many bookstores and libraries today, certain areas are set aside for such genre works as detective novels, science fiction novels, spy novels, westerns, and romances. These novels have certain characteristics that make it possible to classify them as being in certain genres, though there is often a good deal of mixing of genres—as in a science fiction novel that involves a murder mystery.

Genre novels tend to have certain kinds of heroes and heroines and villains, to take place in particular locations, to have specific kinds of plots, and so on. John Cawelti deals with this matter in his book *The Six-Gun Mystique* (1971):

> All cultural products contain a mixture of two elements: conventions and inventions. Conventions are elements which are known to both the creator and his audience beforehand—they consist of things like favorite plots, stereotyped characters, accepted ideas, commonly known metaphors and other linguistic devices, etc. Inventions, on the other hand, are elements which are uniquely imagined by the creator such as new kinds of characters, ideas or linguistic forms. (p. 37)

James Joyce's *Finnegan's Wake* would be at the inventive end of the spectrum and genre works at the other, even though formula works often contain many elements of invention, and vice versa.

TABLE 9.1 Conventions in Popular Culture Genres

Element	Western	Detective	Spy	Science Fiction
Time	1800s	present	present	future
Place	American West	city	world	space
Hero	cowboy	detective	agent	spaceman
Heroine	schoolmarm	damsel	spy	spacegal
Villains	outlaws	killers	moles	aliens
Plot	restore law and order	find killer	find mole	repel aliens
Theme	justice	discovery of killer	save free world	save world
Costume	cowboy hat	raincoat	suit	high-tech clothes
Locomotion	horse	beat-up car	sports car	spaceship
Weapon	six-gun	pistol and fists	pistol with silencer	ray gun

Table 9.1 lists a number of the most common genres—westerns, tough-guy detective novels, spy novels, and science fiction novels—along with some of their commonly used conventions. There are, of course, many other plots, kinds of villains, and themes possible in each of these genres, but the table gives some sense of what Cawelti means by the term *conventions*.

Genres and Formulas

I make a distinction between genres and formulas. The term *genre* means "class" or "kind" and is used to refer to the kind of texts mentioned in Table 9.1. Within a given genre, however, there may be a number of different formulas. For example, there are three main formulas found in the detective genre:

1. *The classical formula* employs heroes like Sherlock Holmes and Hercule Poirot, who are not members of a police force but, because of their brilliant minds, are used by the police. They are usually "consulting" detectives, seldom are at risk and seldom involved sexually with women.

2. *The tough-guy formula* features heroes like Sam Spade and Mike Hammer, private investigators who have ambivalent relations with the police. They

are often involved with women and also are often in danger (cynics might say the two go together).

3. *The procedural formula* has heroes like Dick Tracy, who belong to a police force and use the resources of the police (laboratories and so on) to track down criminals.

Whatever their formulas, detective novels don't usually have subplots; everything focuses on catching the criminal—usually a killer. In these novels the hero usually is tested, is in conflict with others (often superiors on the force as well as criminal elements), and has to overcome numerous antagonists in order to triumph.

There always has to be some jeopardy, some question about whether the hero or heroine will triumph, to hold the reader's attention. Although we may be certain that Hercule Poirot will eventually discover who the killer (or killers) is (or are), how he does so becomes the interesting thing. The same may be said of all popular culture genres: We may have a pretty good idea what will happen in the end, but we don't know how the heroes will triumph and achieve their goals.

Now that I have offered some ideas about what novels are like (that is, "literary" or "elite" culture novels) and how they differ from popular culture or genre novels, I would like to examine a few pages from a significant genre novel to show how authors use the various devices at their disposal to create the effects they want.

Narrative Techniques in *I, the Jury*

Mickey Spillane's *I, the Jury* (1947) was one of the most popular "tough-guy" detective novels of the 1940s, selling more than 6 million copies; it ranks as one of the best-selling books ever published in the United States. In this section I will examine some of the narrative techniques Spillane uses in the opening and concluding pages of this book. Here are the first few sentences of *I, the Jury*:

> I shook the rain from my hat and walked into the room. Nobody said a word. They stepped back politely and I could feel their eyes on me. Pat Chambers was standing by the door to the bedroom trying to steady Myrna. The girl's body was racking with dry sobs. I walked over and put my arm around her.

From a stylistic perspective, the first thing we notice is that this story is told in the first person, from what is called a first-person participant point of view.

The hero of the story, who plays a major role in it, tells us what happens more or less as it happens. (There are other possibilities Spillane could have used. He could have had his hero be a first-person observer, someone more or less on the sidelines, telling what happened. Or he could have written in the third person and used a third-person omniscient, selectively omniscient, or objective storyteller.)

One problem with the first-person participant point of view is that we know immediately that the narrator will survive any dangers he faces in the story, because he is telling the story. This tends to negate one element of suspense, although of course there is other excitement generated by watching the hero track down the killer and escape from traps that have been set for him.

We know right away in this opening scene that something terrible has happened. Everyone is quiet and a woman is sobbing hysterically, her body "racking with dry sobs." We see the hero acting tenderly as he comforts her. There are police in the room, which suggests, given the conventions of the murder mystery and the air of solemnity, that there has been a murder. Later we learn the hero's name, Mike, and that he is known to the police, given that Pat Chambers, whom we assume is one of the police, calls him by name.

In the paragraphs that follow, we learn that a character named Jack Williams, a policeman, has been killed. Williams had saved Mike Hammer's life during World War II (and lost an arm in doing so) and was Hammer's best friend. Hammer notices that a chair with Jack's revolver on it has been moved and asks about it. The police say they didn't move it. Then Hammer offers an insight into the nature of the killer:

> That chair was over there by the bed. I've been here often enough to remember that much. After the killer shot Jack, he pulled himself toward the chair. But the killer didn't leave after the shooting. He stood here and watched him grovel on the floor in agony. Jack was after that gun, but he never reached it. He could have if the killer didn't move it. The trigger-happy bastard must have stood by the door laughing while Jack tried to make his last play. He kept pulling the chair back, inch by inch, until Jack gave up. Tormenting a guy who's been through all sorts of hell, laughing. This was no ordinary murder, Pat. It's as cold-blooded and deliberate as I ever saw one. I'm going to get the one that did this. (p. 6)

We learn several things here. We learn that Hammer is perceptive—he notices that Jack's chair has been moved, something the police missed. He also is able to characterize the murderer as a "cold-blooded" and sadistic "bastard." When Hammer vows vengeance, Chambers tells him he's got to "go easy." Hammer replies, "We'll work together as usually, but in the homestretch, I'm going to pull the trigger." He adds that he's not going to let the killer hire expensive lawyers, get off by arguing temporary insanity or having to defend himself, and wind up as "the hero."

Several paragraphs later, Hammer makes a pledge to his dead friend:

> I'm going to get the louse that killed you. He won't sit in the chair. He won't hang. He will die exactly as you died, with a .45 slug in the gut, just a little below the belly button. No matter who it is, Jack, I'll get the one. Remember, no matter who it is, I promise. (pp. 7-8)

Thus in the first four pages of the novel we have Mike Hammer pledged to kill the person who killed his best friend so brutally—no matter who it is. We have a sadistic, cold-blooded murderer to contend with, and we have a smart, tough private detective who, he tells us later, isn't afraid to break an arm or play a bit fast and loose with the law to accomplish his task.

In the course of his investigation, Hammer meets and falls for a beautiful psychiatrist, Charlotte Manning. Here is how Spillane describes her in a very important passage:

> She strode provocatively across the room and back toward me. Under the dress her body was superb. . . . She was slimmer, really, her waist thin, but her shoulders broad. Her breasts were laughing things that were firmly in place, although I could see no strap marks of a restraining bra. Her legs were encased in sheer nylons and set in high heels, making her almost as tall as I was. Beautiful legs. They were strong looking, shapely. . . .
>
> "Well, do you like it?" she asked again.
>
> "Lovely. And you know it." I grinned at her. "You remind me of something."
>
> "What?"
>
> "A way of torturing a guy." (p. 60)

In the context of this scene, in which Hammer is being sexually aroused, we don't pay much attention to the word *torture*, but it turns out that Spillane has actually given readers a clue. Charlotte Manning is someone who "tortures" people and the killer also was someone who tortured people. And it turns out, ironically, that Charlotte Manning is the killer.

At the end of the book, in the last two pages, is a famous scene in which Hammer confronts Manning and explains how he figured out that she killed Jack Williams. As he talks, in an extended monologue, Manning starts stripping. The description of her striptease is given in italics. Hammer makes his case. He explains that no jury would convict Manning because her alibis are too good, and that it won't be necessary to worry about smart lawyers brainwashing juries. He then says, in the best tradition of American vigilantism:

> "No, Charlotte, I'm the jury now, and the judge, and I have a promise to keep. Beautiful as you are, as much as I almost loved you, I sentence you to death."
>
> *(Her thumbs hooked in the fragile silk of the panties and pulled them down. She stepped out of them as delicately as one coming from a bathtub. She was completely naked now. A sun-tanned goddess giving herself to her lover. With arms outstretched she walked toward me. Lightly, her tongue ran over her lips,*

making them glisten with passion. The smell of her was like an exhilarating
perfume. Slowly, a sigh escaped her, making the hemispheres of her breasts quiver.
She leaned forward to kiss me, her arms going out to encircle my neck.)

The roar of the .45 shook the room. Charlotte staggered back a step.
Her eyes were a symphony of incredulity, an unbelieving witness to the
truth. Slowly, she looked down at the ugly swelling in her naked belly
where the bullet went in. A thin trickle of blood welled out. (p. 173)

After he shoots her, Hammer discovers that Manning had a gun ready
to use on the table behind him, and that she was planning to blow his
brains out. (This fact is intended as justification for Hammer's killing
her.) The book ends with Charlotte gasping, incredulously, "How
c-could you?" and Hammer answering, "It was easy."

We can see that there is a symmetry in *I, the Jury*. Charlotte Manning
shot Mike Hammer's best friend through the stomach and Hammer
shoots her through the stomach. He has honored his pledge to avenge
his friend's murder. He justifies shooting Manning with a vigilante's
explanation: She would have gotten off if brought to trial. In addition,
she was planning on killing him, if he had let her embrace him.

The combination of violence and sexual titillation and teasing in *I, the
Jury* must have struck a responsive chord in the reading public, because
it was a great success from a sales point of view. But the book reflects
also a diffuse kind of anxiety about female sexuality: Men have to be very
careful, it suggests, because women will use their sexual attractiveness
to distract or even destroy men when it suits their purposes. The book's
enormous popularity suggests that it tapped something very basic in the
American psyche—a fear of women and a sense that individuals, at
times, have to take the law into their own hands. This latter notion is still
alive in U.S. society, as the militia movement shows.

A Concluding Note
on Fantasy and Reality

When we look at novels and other texts analytically, we focus on the
various techniques authors use to create the effects they want. From what
point of view (that is, in which person) do they write? How do they use
language? What are their descriptions like? What is their dialogue like?
How do they combine dialogue, description, and action?

It isn't too far-fetched to think of writers as being like military officers who employ various strategies to win a war—the war being creating a book that people will find worth reading. Writers want to "entertain" their readers in the best sense of the word—they want to create characters who are interesting and worth following, want to have these characters interact with one another in ways that amuse us, teach us something about life, and give us something to think about.

People read popular culture genre fiction for amusement and entertainment primarily, but I would like to suggest that they get more out of these texts than they might imagine. All texts teach us things, whether about human personality, about motivation, about morality, or about the nature of love. We read, in part, to escape from our day-to-day existences and to live vicariously through other people—to have adventures, to meet interesting people of all kinds, and to gain insights that will help us live better lives.

Bruno Bettelheim (1976) makes an interest point relating to the matter of fantasy and reality: Fairy tales are fantasies, but fantasies are necessary for children (and for adults as well, I would add); they may be works of imagination, but they convey truths—about human personality and the like. Bettelheim explains that it is a mistake to believe that a rich fantasy life interferes with an individual's ability to cope with reality. In fact, just the opposite happens to be the case. People who are compulsive generally are focused upon a very narrow range of topics; these people do not have rich fantasy lives, but rather they tend to be tied to some anxiety-provoking or wish-fulfilling daydream. Fairy tales, on the other hand, generate a rich variety of fantasies that help a child avoid getting stuck in the confines of daydreams that focus on a narrow range of preoccupations.

What Bettelheim says about children and fairy tales can also be applied to adults and the fictional texts of all kinds that they read. These texts provide us with ways to escape from our personal preoccupations and open us up to a broader sense of possibilities. Ironically, the richer and more varied our fantasy lives, the better we can cope with reality.

The central point of Orson Welles' broadcast, it seems to me, is that the frame that defines apocalypse as a useful fiction can never be made secure *enough*. H. G. Wells' novel may seem to be sufficiently unambiguous as a fiction, but, as with all apocalypses, the frame of fictionality is unstable. There simply is no safe way, Orson Welles implies, to play with apocalyptic fire. When the message "this is a play" is all that stands between social order and social chaos, then those who wish to create chaos may attempt to exploit the weakness of the fictive frame. And what the educated take as fiction may turn out to be more like a magical incantation, whose description of a non-existent state of affairs brings that state of affairs into being. This was, indeed, what actually happened with Orson Welles' broadcast. . . . The "worlds" that are at war in Welles' broadcast are, in fact, the worlds of fiction and reality; and the central action of Welles' drama was its reception, its planned misapprehension by much of its audience, designed to demonstrate the danger and possible success of more sinister contemporary conspiracies whose "fictions" would never be acknowledged as such.

Gary Saul Morson, "The War of the Well(e)s" (1984, p. 173)

10

Radio Narratives

A Case Study of the War of the Worlds *Script*

R adio has been described, as I have suggested earlier, as "the theater of the mind." What this means is that when we listen to a narrative on radio, we use our minds to visualize (to see with the mind's eye, that is) or imagine what the characters look like, what they are like, where they are, and what they are doing. Consider how simple it is to put on a radio drama. The basic elements are (a) actors, (b) a script telling a story of some kind, (c) music, and (d) sound effects.

Because radio relies on the ability of people to imagine things in their minds, and because, given the right cues (by the use of voice, sound effects, and music), we can imagine anything, radio can tell the most incredible stories. And the cost of producing radio narratives, relative to that of film or television, for example, is trivial.

One of the most famous illustrations of this is a famous ad to promote advertising on radio that was written by Stan Freberg, in which a gigantic maraschino cherry is dropped into Lake Michigan as thousands applaud. The script for the ad reads as follows:

FREBERG   Okay people, now when I give the cue, I want the 700-foot mountain of whipped cream to roll into Lake Michigan, which has been drained and filled with hot chocolate. Then the Royal Canadian Air Force will fly overhead, towing a ten-ton maraschino cherry which will be dropped into the whipped cream to the cheering of 25,000 extras.

FREBERG   All right, cue the mountain.

SFX   *(CREAKS, GROANS, PROLONGED SPLASH)*

FREBERG   Cue the Air Force.

SFX   *(PROPELLERS ROAR INTO AND PAST MIKE, WING STRUTS WHINE)*

FREBERG   Cue the maraschino cherry.

SFX   *(SCREAMING, WHISTLING FALL, AND LARGE PLOP)*

FREBERG   Okay, 25,000 cheering extras.

SFX   *(PROLONGED AND TUMULTUOUS OVATION)*

FREBERG   Now—you want to try that on television?

SPONSOR   Wel-l-l-l

FREBERG   You see, radio's a very special medium.

SPONSOR   Doesn't television stretch the imagination?

FREBERG   Up to 21 inches—yes.

SOURCE: Reprinted by permission of Stan Freberg, Freberg Ltd. Los Angeles, CA.

Today Freberg would have to change the last line, given that television sets are made in much larger sizes now than when he wrote the ad, but his point is still valid: You can do things with radio that you can't do with television or film—even with the new technologies that have been developed. That's because the images a radio presentation generates in our minds are our own, private, personal ones. The images we see on television and in films, on the other hand, are always mediated—that is, they are always someone else's images.

The only limitation radio faces is that of the human imagination, and that is boundless. We must recognize, also, that the human voice is an incredibly powerful instrument. Performers can create all kinds of effects by their use of accents, by the tones in which they speak, by the softness or loudness of their voices, and by using devices that affect the sounds of their voices and generate special effects, such as echoes. (This also applies to film and television and other media as well.)

There are, for example, "educated voices," voices that sound as though they must belong to educated or professional people. We can suggest socioeconomic class, geographic region, and race by accent, among other things. So the human voice is a remarkable instrument and can be used to give listeners all kinds of information that need not necessarily be stated. But using dialogue, music, and sound, script writers must make certain that their audiences understand and can easily follow what is happening in their stories. That means that stories have to be written in a rather simple manner and that the characters or a narrator must provide information to audiences about motivation and actions.

Terms Used in Radio Production

Radio scripts, as Freberg's ad shows, are relatively simple compared, for example, with movie and television scripts—which must tie visual information to the dialogue. Contemporary radio scripts conventionally have two columns. One column, about an inch or so in width, is for the names of the characters or performers; everything in this column is printed in capital letters. It is also used to denote sound effects (SFX) and for music. The rest of the page is used for the dialogue and for information, usually in parentheses and all caps, about how the lines are to be read or what form the various effects should take. Table 10.1 lists some of the technical terms generally used in producing radio scripts.

The *War of the Worlds* Panic

The famous (or should I say infamous) Mercury Theatre on the Air broadcast of *The War of the Worlds* took place on the night before Halloween, October 30, 1938. The script was written by Howard Koch, who made an adaptation for radio of H. G. Wells's *The War of the Worlds* for Orson Welles and his group of actors and actresses. This broadcast led to a nationwide panic. As Hadley Cantril, a social scientist from Prince-

TABLE 10.1 Radio Script Terms

Fade in	The sound starts from nothing and rises to normal speaking level. This is the way programs and scenes generally start.
Fade out	The sound becomes fainter and fainter and gradually disappears. Most programs and scenes end with this direction.
Cross-fade	One sound fades out while another fades in.
Sneak	Sound is slowly faded in, under ongoing sound.
Under	Music or other sounds are soft and heard "under" the dialogue.
Over	Music or other sounds are loud and dominate the dialogue.
Up	The sound rises in loudness.
Out	Music or other sound stops being heard.
Up and out	Music or other sound rises in loudness and then stops (the reverse is *under and out*).
Sting	A short piece of music, often a dissonant chord, is used to shock listeners and suggest that something important is happening or about to happen.
Filter	An electronic device modifies a speaker's voice in some manner.
On mike	Performer is at the microphone.
Off mike	Performer is away from the microphone.
Sound effects	Various sounds are used to create impressions, such as to suggest time; to indicate a person is opening or closing a door, entering or leaving a room; to suggest a mood; and to indicate what the weather is like.

ton University, describes in his book *The Invasion From Mars: A Study in the Psychology of Panic* (1966):

> Long before the broadcast had ended, people all over the United States were praying, crying, fleeing frantically to escape death from the Martians. Some ran to rescue loved ones. Others telephoned farewells or warnings, hurried to inform neighbors, sought information from newspapers or radio stations, summoned ambulances and police cars. At least six million people heard the broadcast. At least a million of them were frightened or disturbed. (p. 47)

This is a remarkable testimonial to the power of a narrative, in this case one broadcast by the mass media, to affect large numbers of people in profound ways. Cantril estimates that the figure of a million people is probably quite conservative.

Cantril believes that the panic created by the broadcast was tied to anxiety and fear that were "latent in the general population" (p. 202); the broadcast basically activated this latent anxiety and functioned like a match that set off a bomb waiting to explode. He ends his book by noting the need for education, asserting that people need to learn how to question what they hear; he also argues that we must do something about the social inequalities that lead to panics and other forms of social disorientation.

The Openings of the
War of the Worlds Script and Book

A reproduction of Howard Koch's adaptation of Wells's book occupies 40 pages of Cantril's book. It appears there in the format of scripts for film and television dramas, with the name of the performer or speaker in capitals in the center of the page and the dialogue extending to both margins.

The script takes a number of the more important scenes in Wells's book and dramatizes them. It starts off with Orson Welles being introduced by an announcer. Here are the first sentences from the script read on the air by Orson Welles, followed by the first words of Wells's novel.

We know now that in the early years of the twentieth century this world was being watched closely by intelligences greater than man's and yet as mortal as his own. We know now that as human beings busied themselves about their various concerns they were scrutinized and studied, perhaps almost as narrowly as a man with a microscope might scrutinize the transient creatures that swarm and multiply in a drop of water. (in Cantril, 1966, p. 4)

No one would have believed in the last years of the nineteenth century that this world was being watched keenly and closely by intelligences greater than man's and yet as mortal as his own; that as men busied themselves about their various concerns they were scrutinized and studied, perhaps almost as narrowly as a man with a microscope might scrutinize the transient creatures that swarm and multiply in a drop of water. (Wells, 1898/1964, p. 1)

Basically, the openings are the same, except that the script uses the phrase "we know now" twice instead of Wells's rather impersonal "No one would have believed." The drama is set in motion by this opening.

The script then cuts out a bit of Wells's language that follows this passage, and then repeats his chilling words that came next in a marvelous bit of writing. In Wells's (1898/1964) novel:

Yet across the gulf of space, minds that are to our minds as ours are to those of the beasts that perish, intellects vast and cool and unsympathetic regarded this earth with envious eyes, and slowly and surely drew their plans against us. And early in the twentieth century came the great disillusionment. (p. 7)

The Koch script version of this passage is very similar:

Yet across an immense ethereal gulf, minds that are to our minds as ours are to the beasts in the jungle, intellects vast, cool and unsympathetic regarded this earth with envious eyes and slowly and surely drew their plans against us. In the thirty-ninth year of the twentieth century came the great disillusionment. (in Cantril, 1966, pp. 4-5)

The only important change here is Koch's substitution of "in the thirty-ninth year of the twentieth century" (or 1938, the year of the broadcast) for "early in the twentieth century." The script then adds some further information:

It was near the end of October. Business was better. The war scare was over. More men were back at work. Sales were picking up. On this particular evening, October 30, the Crossley service estimated that thirty-two million people were listening in on their radios. (in Cantril, 1966, p. 5)

H. G. Wells makes use of comparisons to create his effects. We are told that the Martians are to humans as humans are to microbes in a drop of water, and that their minds are to ours as ours are to "the beasts that perish." And these Martian minds are "vast and cool and unsympathetic." These lines generate a diffuse sense of paranoia, as it is suggested that we are being watched and the watchers are not very nice.

It may be argued that in his choice of words here Wells actually has made a minor mistake in his writing. He describes the Martians as having minds that are "cool and unsympathetic," suggesting that the Martians lack emotions, yet he then says they "regarded this earth with envious eyes," suggesting that they do, in fact, have emotions. Perhaps his use of the word "cool" could be taken to indicate the possibility of the Martians' having some emotions. Later in the book, however, he describes them as being heads with tentacles that, vampirelike, suck blood, and he says that as they have no organs, they have no emotions.

Our bodies are half made up of glands and tubes and organs, occupied in turning heterogeneous food into blood. The digestive processes and their reactions upon the nervous system sap our strength and colour our minds. Men go happy or miserable as they have healthy or unhealthy livers, or sound gastric glands. But the Martians were lifted above all these organic fluctuations of mood and emotion. (Wells, 1898/1964, p. 112)

The Interruptions

In the script, after Orson Welles finishes his opening monologue, an announcer gives a weather forecast and then switches to the Meridian Room of the Hotel Park Plaza in New York for some music. The script then has a series of interruptions in which "a special bulletin from the Intercontinental Radio News" tells of a Professor Farrell in an observatory in Chicago observing some explosions on Mars.

The script switches back and forth between the music at the Hotel Park Plaza and interruptions in which various authorities are interviewed and the radio overhears, so to speak, events being acted out. An announcer interrupts the music to bring an interview by reporter Carl Phillips with Professor Richard Pierson, a "famous astronomer" at Princeton University. Pierson, the hero of the story, is played by Orson Welles. Later on, reports from other professors are given and the news that a "huge, flaming object" has fallen in a field 11 miles from Princeton University. Phillips interviews a folksy farmer, Mr. Wilmuth, on whose farmland the object has fallen.

Phillips and Pierson are on hand when the creatures in the space capsule start unscrewing its hatch and then show themselves. Phillips describes it:

> Good heavens, something's wriggling out of the shadow like a grey snake. Now it's another one, and another. They look like tentacles to me. There, I can see the thing's body. It's large as a bear and it glistens like wet leather. But that face. It . . . it's indescribable. I can hardly force myself to keep looking at it. The eyes are black and gleam like a serpent. The mouth is V-shaped with saliva dripping from its rimless lips that seem to quiver and pulsate. (in Cantril, 1966, p. 16)

The script at this point indicates various sound effects, such as clanking sounds, hissing sounds, humming sounds, shouts from crowds, and explosions, to give listeners an idea of what is happening and establish a mood of panic and terror in the people involved with the Martians.

Next there are a couple of scenes in which military forces attempt to destroy the Martians, but are unsuccessful. The Martians have heat rays and discharge thick black smoke that kills everyone. The Martians, in five big machines, are devastating all that lies before them. And more Martian space cylinders are falling all over the country. People are fleeing in boats, the streets are jammed with confused people, who are "falling like flies." An announcer describes the black smoke coming toward him. He says that it's "100 yards away . . . it's 50 feet . . . ." The script then cuts to an operator trying to reach someone:

> 2X2L calling CQ. . . .
> 2X2L calling CQ. . . .

2X2L calling CQ. . . . New York.
Isn't there anyone on the air?
Is there anyone. . . .
2X2L—— (in Cantril, 1966, p. 31)

This character is silenced, and we have the idea that the Martians are killing everyone. This leads to an intermission. An announcer indicates to listeners of the program that they are hearing Orson Welles and the Mercury Theatre in an original dramatization of *The War of the Worlds*. After the break, Pierson becomes the dominant figure.

The Structure of the Text

The first half of the broadcast, leading to the break, is full of descriptions of the Martians landing, what they look like, and "eyewitness accounts" of the terror they spread. The second half of the broadcast is devoted, mostly, to dialogue between Pierson and a stranger, an artillery man, which is taken from a chapter in the book titled "The Man From Putney Hill." In this chapter we find discussions of the notion that the Martians are bringing an end to the world. The artillery man tells of his plan to live underground, in the sewers of New York, with "a bunch of strong men together. No weak ones, that rubbish, out" (in Cantril, 1966, p. 39). Pierson, in disgust, leaves the stranger. Immediately after this, the story is brought to a rapid conclusion, much as it is in the book.

Wells (1898/1964) has the Martians howling, "Ulla, ulla, ulla" as they lay dying. He then gives us the image of a dog:

I heard a yelping chorus and saw, first a dog with a piece of putrescent red meat in his jaws coming headlong towards me, and then a pack of starving mongrels in pursuit of him. (p. 148)

In the radio script, this is rendered as follows:

I stood alone on Times Square. I caught sight of a lean dog running down Seventh Avenue with a piece of dark brown meat in his jaws, and a pack of starving mongrels at his heels. (in Cantril, 1966, p. 40)

A couple of paragraphs later, the script comes to a conclusion with a mention of the bacteria that killed the Martians. We find Pierson in his study at Princeton, writing his memoirs about the Martian invasion. Then Orson Welles makes an announcement to end the episode:

> This is Orson Welles, ladies and gentlemen, out of character to assure you that the *War of the Worlds* has no further significance than as the holiday offering it was intended to be. The Mercury Theatre's own radio version of dressing up in a sheet and jumping out of a bush and saying Boo! (in Cantril, 1966, p. 42)

He adds a few more lines about Halloween, and the program ends. This announcement was not very effective in averting panic; by the time Welles made it, huge numbers of impressionable listeners had been frightened, and many were panic-stricken.

When we look at the *War of the Worlds* script today, it seems amazing that a text so simple could have the effects it had. The program's production values were quite modest: It included a few sound effects here and there, and some crowd noises, but nothing very difficult to do at all. The play's power came from the imagination of its audience, from the audience's ability to "see" the characters and "participate" emotionally in the activities being described. This text functioned as it did (and all stories, plays, movies, and so on function as they do) because of our "willing suspicion of disbelief."

In this radio play, most of the horror comes from the descriptions of the Martians and their death rays and other instruments of destruction. It includes some action, in the scenes of the military trying to destroy the Martians and instead being wiped out, but the second half has no real action to speak of. Pierson talks with an artillery man who has crazed ideas about how to survive in the sewers of New York, and then he sees the dogs with chunks of the Martians, who have been killed by bacteria. Bacteria, in fact, are introduced in the very first paragraph of the book and in the opening speech of the play, so the story has a kind of circularity.

A Personal Note

I grew up in the 1930s and 1940s, when the radio was full of wonderful shows every week—*The Lone Ranger; Jack Armstrong* (the All-American Boy); *Mr. Keen, Tracer of Lost Persons; The FBI in Peace and War; The Green Hornet; Counterspy.* And when I was in high school in Boston, at Roxbury Memorial High School for Boys, I took a class in speech that took us to a radio station, where we acted out scripts every week—along with an organist, who provided the "mood" music. It amazed me how little was needed to put on a decent radio drama.

Radio drama has now been replaced, for the most part, by television, and although television adds something to storytelling, it also takes a great deal away, because we no longer have to use our imaginations to visualize the stories we hear in our minds. I think we lost something valuable when radio drama was displaced by TV.

The community in the western can be seen as a positive force, a movement of refinement, order and local democracy into the wilds, or as a harbinger of corruption in the form of Eastern values which threaten frontier ways. . . . Thus central to the form, we have a philosophical dialectic, an ambiguous cluster of meanings and attitudes that provide the traditional thematic structure of the genre. This shifting ideological play can be described through a series of antinomies, so:

THE WILDERNESS	CIVILIZATION
The Individual	*The Community*
freedom	restriction
honour	institutions
self-knowledge	illusions
integrity	compromise
self-interest	social-responsibility
solipsism	democracy
Nature	*Culture*
purity	corruption
experience	knowledge
empiricism	legalism
pragmatism	idealism
brutalization	refinement
savagery	humanity
The West	*The East*
America	Europe
the frontier	America
equality	class
agrarianism	industrialism
tradition	change
the past	the future

In scanning this grid, if we compare the tops and tails of each subsection, we can see the ambivalence at work at its outer limits: the West, for example, rapidly moves from being the spearhead of manifest destiny to the retreat of ritual. What we are dealing with here is no less than a national-world view: underlying the whole complex is the grave problem of identity that has special meaning for Americans.

Jim Kitses, *Horizons West* (1969, pp. 11-12)

11

Film Narratives

F ilm is different from other media in a number of different ways, which means the narratives we find on film have some differences that are worth considering. A film is basically a series of photographic images projected at 24 frames per second, with accompanying sound (some of which is dialogue) and music used to tell a story of some kind. Audiences, through the willing suspension of disbelief, become emotionally affected by these images, sounds, and music, and also often identify with characters in films and learn something about themselves and about life in the process.

Distinctive Aspects of
Film as a Medium

When we see a film in a theater, the room is dark, we are in a public space, and our attention is focused on huge images projected onto a screen and the accompanying sounds—music, spoken words, and various effects. When we see a film on television, the viewing situation is not the same; we view it on a video screen, usually in a lighted room and in our own homes—where there may be interruptions, people talking in the background, phone calls being made, and so on.

The screen ratios are also different between movies and television, generally speaking. With films we have the following screen ratios:

- *Old films:* 1.3 times as wide as high
- *Ordinary more contemporary films:* 1.85 times as wide as high
- *Ultrawide films:* 2.3 times as wide as high

The television screen is also 1.3 times as wide as it is high, which means that when we watch some films on television, the images have to be cropped or there are thick black bands on the top and the bottom of the image to duplicate the 1.85:1 ratio. In addition, because of time limitations and commercials, films are often cut to fit certain time slots. We don't generally see films on commercial broadcast television as coherent texts, but rather as a series of miniscenes between commercials.

Also, of course, the images on television are much smaller than they are in a movie theater, and the quality of sound is not as good. Altogether, the considerable differences between seeing a movie in a theater and seeing it on television combine to lessen the film's impact, though it still can be significant.

Film is further different from other media in that it generally has a longer continuous period of time in which to develop a story. The average film lasts between 90 and 120 minutes—much longer than most television programs and longer than many theater productions.

Joseph M. Boggs discusses the differences between film and other media in his book *The Art of Watching Films* (1978):

> Like the drama, film communicates visually through dramatic action, gesture and expression, and verbally through dialogue. Like music and poetry, film utilizes complex and subtle rhythms, and, like poetry in particular, it communicates through images, metaphors, and symbols. Like pantomime, film concentrates upon a moving image, and like the dance, that moving image has certain rhythmic qualities. Finally, like the novel, film has the ability to manipulate time and space, to expand or compress them, and to move back and forth freely within the wide borders of these two dimensions. (p. 4)

Boggs calls attention to the way film duplicates many of the techniques found in other media and combines them into one complex and powerful medium. Images, symbols, metaphors, and other such phenomena require, as we have seen, some kind of knowledge on the part of the reader, who is, in this case, a viewer.

Film also has a visceral impact that goes beyond what the intellect makes of things, and that is because of the power of images. (Television also often has a visceral impact, but it is not as powerful as film in this respect.) Images are resonant and call up in us all kinds of unrecognized and suppressed feelings. Images can also make us feel and seemingly experience widely different emotions, such as disgust, intense fear, and sexual desire. One theory that has been used to explain this power of film is that of the montage, which is the subject I turn to now.

Montage

One of the most celebrated theorists of montage, Sergei Eisenstein (1975), explains the way montage functions in an essay titled "Word and Image." Eisenstein says that the filmmaker must present a narrative that is not only logically connected but also has a powerful emotional impact. That is where montage comes in. He describes montage by saying that any two pieces of film *"of any kind, placed together, inevitably combine into a new concept, a new quality, arising out of that juxtaposition"* (p. 4). The way this works, he goes on to explain, is by carrying the viewer along with the emotions of the creator:

> The strength of montage resides in this, that it includes in the creative process the emotions and mind of the spectator. The spectator is compelled to proceed along that selfsame creative road that the author traveled in creating the image. The spectator not only sees the represented elements of the finished work, but also experiences the dynamic process of the emergence and assembly of the image just as it was experienced by the author. (p. 32)

The film image, and the combination of film images that create montages, then *compels* the viewer to experience certain emotions and feelings.

These montage elements, Eisenstein (1975) continues in an essay titled "Synchronization of Senses," have an impact on every sense. He quotes from the Goncourt *Journals* some lines about an athletic arena:

> In the deep shadow of the two ends of the hall, the scintillation of the buttons and sword hilts of the policemen.
>   The glistening limbs of wrestlers darting into the full light.—Challenging eyes.—Hands slapping flesh in coming to grips.—Sweat smelling of the wild beast.—Paleness blending with blonde moustaches.—Bruised flesh growing pink.—Backs sweating like the stone walls of a steam bath.—Advancing by dragging on their knees.—Whirling on their heads, etc. etc. (p. 72)

This prose has a number of direct appeals to the senses, which Eisenstein lists for us:

1. The sense of *touch* (backs sweating like the stone walls of a steam bath)
2. The sense of *smell* (sweat smelling of the wild beast)
3. The sense of *sight* including both *light* (the deep shadow and the glistening limbs of wrestlers darting into the full light; the buttons and sword hilts of the policemen gleaming in the deep shadow) and *color* (paleness blending with blonde moustaches, bruised flesh growing pink)
4. The sense of *hearing* (hands slapping flesh)
5. The sense of *movement* (advancing on knees, whirling on their heads)
6. *Pure emotion*, or drama (challenging eyes)

All of this leads Eisenstein to suggest that there is no appreciable difference between purely visual montage and montage that links various spheres of feeling together in other art forms.

The short passage quoted and analyzed by Eisenstein shows how even a relatively simple verbal text can generate sense experiences. Film can do so also, but with even greater intensity and power. This happens only when a film is successful, of course. But even second-rate directors and flawed or poor films often generate powerful effects in viewers; the element of psychic compulsion felt by those attending films and generated by filmmakers (if only for an interlude of an hour and a half or so) is an important aspect of watching films.

John G. Cawelti
on the Western Formula

The western film I will be discussing here is one of the most famous ever made: *High Noon*. Before I discuss it, however, I would like to say something about what westerns are and the formulaic nature of the western as a genre. Cawelti discusses some of the essential attributes of the western in his book *The Six-Gun Mystique* (1971):

1. It must "take place in the West, near the frontier, at a point in history when social order and anarchy are in tension" and must involve "some form of pursuit" (p. 31). The setting—in the American West, with its peculiar terrain (open plains, mountains, and so on)—is crucial, as is the time period, near the end of the frontier, when the West had not been fully civilized. In this setting, the western costume—cowboy hats, boots, and so on—makes sense.

2. It must have what Frank Gruber, a writer of pulp westerns, has described as one of the seven basic plots found in westerns: (a) the Union-Pacific Story, dealing with the construction of a railroad or telegraph or stagecoach line, or the adventures of a wagon train; (b) the Ranch Story, focusing on battles between ranchers and rustlers or cattlemen and sheepmen; (c) the Empire Story, an epic version of the Ranch Story; (d) the Revenge Story; (e) Custer's Last Stand or the Cavalry and Indian Story; (f) the Outlaw Story; or (g) the Marshall Story. Gruber may simplify things a bit, but his list offers a good sense of the nature of most westerns.

3. It must contain certain character types, the most dominant of which are as follows:

The townspeople, or agents of civilization. There are women among the townspeople who tend to be either agents of civilization (the schoolmarms) or sexually alluring and morally ambiguous women (the saloon girls). The townspeople are too weak or cowardly to defend themselves and thus need the hero.

The savages or outlaws. These characters threaten the townspeople with killing and rape. They are lawless, violent, masculine, rootless, and sometimes psychotic.

The hero. This character mediates between the weak townspeople and the savages and outlaws. The hero, Cawelti points out, often has the skills of the savages and outlaws but works for the townspeople.

Cawelti also notes that the western hero is a man with a horse and a gun—a six-shooter, generally—who is forced to act violently, forced to kill, but his violence is disciplined and somehow pure, in part because it is defensive. The hero also tends to be reluctant with words and with women, being more at ease with some group of male companions. Thus the western hero often rejects love and domesticity and the possibility of economic success to keep moving. There is, according to Cawelti, an antithesis between success and honor in the western hero.

We see, then, that there are a number of different conflicts that occur in westerns. As Cawelti explains, "It is possible to have Westerns without Indians and outlaws, but not without somebody playing the role of the savage, for the antithesis between the townspeople and savagery is the source of plots" (p. 53).

The town, Cawelti adds, creates a dilemma for the hero: The town offers love, domesticity, and respectability, but it demands repression and requires the sacrifice of spontaneity, individuality, and freedom. Thus the hero generally finds himself torn in two directions, with divided commitments. This would suggest that there are internal or psychological conflicts within the hero as well as external or physical conflicts in westerns.

Although the western formula may be relatively simple in outline, the possibilities for creating engaging moral dramas to go along with the fistfights and gun battles are considerable. The possibilities for westerns to have a mythic dimension are many; they often involve heroes whose significance becomes allegorical and resonates loudly in our psyches. It is to this subject we now turn.

TABLE 11.1 Wright's Typology of Western Plots

Plot	Sample Film	Predominant Time	Story Line
Classical	*Shane*	1930-1955	Lone gunfighter saves town or farmers.
Vengeance	*Stagecoach*	1950-1960	Ill-used hero seeks vengeance on villain.
Transitional	*High Noon*	1950-1953	Hero and heroine defend justice but are rejected by society.
Professional	*Rio Bravo*	1958-1970	Professional fighters take jobs for money.

Will Wright's Structural Study of the Western

In this section I offer a brief overview of some of the main ideas presented by Will Wright in his influential study of popular western films, *Sixguns and Society* (1975), which deals with the western's mythic nature and structure. Wright suggests that there are four basic plots used in western movies; I list them here in Table 11.1. In the table, for each plot I also offer the title of a film that exemplifies the plot, give the time period during which that plot was dominant, and outline the plot's basic story line. Wright goes into considerable detail in discussing these four plots, giving brief synopses of a number of the most important films from each category. He points out, of course, that there are often elements from one category in another; there aren't really many "pure" examples of any of the categories.

These four basic plots are important because they are connected, Wright (1975) argues, to social and political institutions. The narrative structure, he asserts, speaks to people and "must reflect the social relationships necessitated by the basic institutions within which they live" (p. 186). He goes on to explain these relationships in some detail, with a particular focus upon economic considerations:

> In the Western, the classical plot shows that the way to achieve such human rewards as friendship, respect, and dignity is to separate yourself from others and use your strength as an autonomous individual to succor them. This plot exists in the context of a restricted but active market economy. The vengeance variation—in the context of a tentative planned economy—weakens the compatibility of the individual and society by showing that the path to respect and love is to separate yourself from others, struggling individually against your many and strong enemies but striving to remember and return to the softer values of marriage and humility. The transition theme, anticipating new social values, argues that love and companionship are available—at the cost of becoming a social outcast—to the individual who stands firmly and righteously against the intolerance of society. Finally, the professional plot—in the context of a corporate economy—argues that companionship and respect are to be achieved only by becoming a skilled technician, who joins an elite group of professionals, accepts any job that is offered, and has loyalty only to the integrity of the team, not to any competing social or community values. (pp. 186-187)

What Wright delineates is, he suggests, a picture of the evolution of American social and economic thought as it works itself out over the years and is reflected, indirectly, in the kinds of westerns that have been produced. What Wright's analysis implies is that as certain beliefs have become dominant in U.S. society, they have been reflected in western films. This has not been done consciously, of course, but has occurred because artists, writers, and creative people of all kinds are attuned to dominant codes and reflect these codes in their work.

The transitional theme is somewhat unique in that Wright sees only three films among the top moneymaking westerns he addresses as fitting into this category: *Broken Arrow, High Noon*, and *Johnny Guitar*. Westerns are important because they have a mythic quality. Myths, Wright suggests, "through their structure, communicate a conceptual order to the members of that society. . . . a myth orders the everyday experiences of its hearers (or viewers) and communicates this order through a formal structure that is understood like language" (p. 17). This is an important point. Myths are generally defined as sacred narratives, and these narratives give people a sense of who they are and how they should live. They are not trivial, and thus neither are the western films that have given form to American myths.

Myths work, Wright continues (taking some ideas from Claude Lévi-Strauss and Ferdinand de Saussure), by setting up bipolar oppositions—because meaning is tied, in essence, to this process. He quotes Saussure on this matter: "Concepts are . . . defined . . . negatively by their relations with other terms of the system. Their most precise characteristic is in being what others are not" (p. 22). Myths work, then, by setting up bipolar oppositions that reflect and reinforce social understandings. They are, Wright suggests, allegories for social action. It is necessary to see both the oppositions found in the myths and the ways they are embodied in narratives—the events that take place in a story and the way the story is resolved.

The basic oppositions that Wright finds in westerns, embodied in their stories and in their visual aspects (clothing, scenery, movements, expressions, and so on), are listed in Table 11.2. These four oppositions are, for Wright, at the core of westerns; the characters and plots involve various combinations and permutations of these oppositions. (We see a somewhat different set of paired oppositions in the Kitses quotation at the opening of this chapter.) Keeping in mind that narratives, by their form, communicate ideas about how we are to see life, how we are to behave, and how we should make sense of experience, let us consider *High Noon* in some detail.

High Noon: A Synopsis

High Noon, which was directed by Fred Zinnemann, was released in 1952. It stars Gary Cooper, who won an Academy Award for his portrayal of Will Kane in the film, and Grace Kelly, who plays the female lead, Amy Fowler Kane. It features a memorable song by Dmitri Tiomkin and Ned Washington, "High Noon (Do Not Forsake Me)," sung by Tex Ritter, and a score by Dmitri Tiomkin, who also won an Oscar.

TABLE 11.2 Oppositions in Westerns

inside society	outside society
good	bad
weak	strong
civilization	wilderness

As the film opens, Will Kane, the sheriff of Hadleyville, is resigning to marry Amy Fowler. After they are married, word reaches town that Frank Miller, who has sworn to kill Kane, has been released from prison and is heading for Hadleyville. (Kane had "cleaned up" Hadleyville and got Miller put in prison.) Miller is expected on the noon train. Kane's friends pressure him to leave town immediately with Amy, and the couple leaves. Kane has second thoughts, however, and, telling his wife he has a job to do, he returns to town to confront Miller and his gang. Amy, who is a Quaker and deplores violence, leaves him. Kane assumes he will get support from the townspeople, but none of them will help him. In a memorable scene, he goes to the town's church during services and asks for help, but nobody is willing to risk his life. Frank Miller arrives at noon and rides into town with three gunmen, and there is a protracted gunfight in which Kane, with Amy's help, manages to kill all the gunmen. After Miller has been killed, the townspeople rush out to the town square to congratulate Kane, but he throws his badge in the dirt in a gesture of contempt and leaves town.

Analyzing *High Noon*

No synopsis can really do justice to the richness of a film—the quality of the acting, the technical aspects of the work, its emotional impact. A synopsis doesn't show us the scenery or the facial expressions of characters, or allow us to be affected by the music or by the kinds of shots used by the director. For our purposes, however, the above synopsis offers a sense of the narrative elements of the film, which are our primary concern.

Wright uses the four oppositions shown in Table 11.2 to interpret *High Noon,* and he points out that something interesting happens in this western: Those who are inside society (the cowardly townspeople) are seen as bad and those outside society (Will and Amy Kane) are seen as good. Kane, like the hero of the classical plot, is a man who is strong, who has special abilities (he's good with a gun), so that opposition still obtains, although Wright suggests that society is now strong and those outside of it (Will and Amy) are weak, a view I find somewhat questionable. After all, Will and Amy confront Frank Miller and his men and kill them. Wright does not see the opposition "wilderness versus civilization" as operating in *High Noon*, though he does find it in the other two films he categorizes as transitional.

I would suggest that there are various kinds of conflict going on in *High Noon* that give the story its resonance. On the most elementary level, we have physical conflict—the matter of the gunfight and the events leading up to it—that generates an enormous amount of tension. Kane tries to get help to reduce the odds against him and cannot, and as he struggles the time is passing and the train is bringing Frank Miller closer to Hadleyville. The title of the film indicates the importance of time in the story, and a number of shots call our attention to passing time. The film runs from 10:40 a.m. to noon, a period that coincides with the actual running time of the film.

Kane's wife, whom he has just married, has deserted him, or so it seems. She is a Quaker and violence is against her religion. Thus there is a moral conflict on her part: Does she follow her religion and let the man she loves be killed, or does she help him, even if it means going against her religious beliefs? At the end of the film we find that she has chosen her love for Kane over her nonviolent principles.

Kane himself struggles with moral issues and, for a brief period, abandons the town, but he quickly returns because he believes he has a moral responsibility to do so. Our understanding of his sense of moral obligation is heightened when we compare his actions with those of the townspeople. The citizens of Hadleyville do not come off very well in this story, from a moral point of view. In essence, they are a cowardly lot; they will not help Kane defend himself, and indirectly themselves, from Frank Miller and his gang. Had Miller killed Kane, it is implied that he would have taken over the town again, and that lawlessness and random violence would prevail.

TABLE 11.3 Conflicts and Oppositions in *High Noon*

Character	Realm	Character
Will Kane	physical	Frank Miller (and gang)
Will Kane as sheriff	moral	people of Hadleyville
Will Kane as husband	moral	Will Kane as sheriff
Amy as wife	moral	Amy as Quaker
Will and Amy	moral	Hadleyville

Table 11.3 presents graphically the different kinds of conflict I have been discussing. We can describe these events spatially. As the plot progresses on the horizontal plane, various characters have to make moral decisions, which can be charted on a vertical plane. Such a chart would show the numbers of events involving ethical dilemmas, which most of the characters in the film do not resolve in what we would consider an acceptable manner.

The only two characters whose decisions are moral find they cannot live in a corrupt and ethically bankrupt community, and thus they leave town. In this sense, *High Noon* is a variation on the standard western plot of having a hero, such as Shane, clean up a town and then leave; in *High Noon*, the hero and his wife leave, though their reasons are different from those of the typical hero.

Bellah, Madsen, Sullivan, Swidler, and Tipton (1985) comment about the significance of the cowboy hero:

> America is . . . the inventor of that most mythic individual hero, the cowboy, who again and again saves a society he can never completely fit into. The cowboy has a special talent—he can shoot straighter and faster than other men—and a special sense of justice. But these characteristics make him so unique that he can never fully belong to society. His destiny is to defend society without ever really joining it. (p. 145)

Thus the western points out a crucial dilemma we find in American society. We need and welcome the cowboy (and modern analogues) because of his remarkable skills, but how do we reconcile his individualism and desire to be free of restraints with society's need for order and decorum and the danger of domestication that comes from falling in love, marrying, and having a family?

The foregoing examination of the western as a genre and *High Noon* in particular suggests the power that narratives have to dramatize and give concrete form to a society's attitudes and beliefs and to help people find meaning in their lives. Narratives, then, are ways societies communicate to their members about some of the important things in life; they are much more than simple entertainments.

Narratives are analogous to rites of initiation, and though aesthetically narratives may be simple, the ways in which they function (psychologically) are quite complex, and their influence and impact are often quite profound. With this in mind, we can see westerns in a new light and recognize that in these texts, societal conflicts and beliefs are given form and resolution. Meaning, of course, has to be elicited; it is never handed to us on a silver platter. If we bother to look at the psychological, political, ethical, and even economic matters underlying western narratives, we can see that there is more significance to the gunfight between Will Kane and Frank Miller and his gang in Hadleyville than we might have imagined.

Like weight bearing walls, personal narratives depend on certain structures to hold them together. Stories told in conversation share common parameters, although they may be put together in contrasting ways and, as a result, point to different interpretations. Events become meaningful because of their placement in a narrative.

Labov's . . . structural approach is paradigmatic: Most investigators cite it, apply it, or use it as a point of departure. . . . Narratives, he argues, have formal properties and each has a function. A "fully formed" one includes six common elements: an abstract (summary of the substance of the narrative), orientation (time, place, situation, participants), complicating action (sequence of events), evaluation (significance and meaning of the action, attitude of the narrator), resolution (what finally happened), and coda (returns the perspective to the present). With these structures, a teller constructs a story from a primary experience and interprets the significance of the events in clauses and embedded evaluation.

Catherine Kohler Riessman,
Narrative Analysis (1993, pp. 18-19)

12

Narratives and
Everyday Life

L et me begin this chapter by offering some suggestions about the differences between fictional narratives and everyday life. By *everyday life* I mean our various activities in the course of a typical day, which include everything from eating to working to entertaining ourselves. Table 12.1 suggests some of the more important differences.

Differences Between
Narratives and Everyday Life

Narratives, as I have been using the term throughout this book, are works of fiction that have sequence; that is, narratives are made-up stories that unfold over time. Everyday life is real; it is the basic stuff, we might say, of our lives. And it goes on, more or less automatically, until we die. We can see, here and there, sequences and narrative elements in our everyday lives, but that is not the same thing as saying they are narratives.

TABLE 12.1 Differences Between Narratives and Everyday Life

Narratives (Mediated)	Everyday Life
fictional	real
have beginning, middle, end	all middle
focused	diffuse
conflict intense, continual	conflict muted, random
each story different	repeat performances
curiosity about resolution	vague goals
eventfulness basic	eventlessness basic
imitate life?	imitates art?

Fictional narratives have closure: They have beginnings, middles, and endings in which the various complications and conflicts that have arisen are resolved. Our everyday lives do not always (or perhaps do not often) have the element of closure—until, that is, we die. Our everyday lives are basically "middles" in which we do our jobs, have our pleasures, and so on. But our deaths are not the resolution of complications (though in some cases they are); instead, they are the more or less abrupt conclusions of our "stories."

Narratives also are much more focused than everyday life; they deal with specific individuals and particular conflicts, problems, threats, or whatever that complicate their lives. Our everyday lives, on the other hand, are relatively routine, and our experiences are not, as a rule, as intense or exciting as those experienced by characters in narrative fiction. Most of us are not spies, police detectives, adventurers, or the like, and though we may have our problems (with colleagues at work, supervisors, spouses, siblings, children, and so on), they are generally not life threatening.

In our ordinary lives, we experience what I call *repeat performances.* Every morning, generally speaking, we have breakfast, and what we eat tends to be somewhat routine. We usually select from a relatively small range of possibilities—juice, cereal, coffee, a donut or toast, maybe eggs (or pancakes or waffles or French toast)—or, in some cases, have the same breakfast over and over again. We need routines or repeat performances (to adopt a theatrical metaphor) to spare us from having to exert energy and make decisions about relatively trivial matters every day. Habits provide security. We want to save our energy for more important decisions. In this respect we differ from the heroes and heroines we follow in narrative fictions; each of their stories (or each episode in the continuing series) is different from the last.

Relatively speaking, everyday life can be described as eventless, whereas the lives of the characters we follow in narrative fictions are eventful and highly charged. In serious dramas characters are faced with various kinds of death and destruction. They have to catch murderers, undertake risky actions, extricate themselves from or get themselves involved in complicated love affairs, and so on. In comedies, the heroes and heroines have to remove themselves from ridiculous messes they create for themselves (or others create for them).

The characters in most genre fictional narratives, whether heroes and heroines in comic books or detective novels or westerns or science fiction adventures, do not have, so to speak, everyday lives; rather, they have lives full of excitement and challenge. Now, interestingly enough, we use narrative fictions to fill up much of the leisure parts of our everyday lives. We derive, I have suggested, numerous gratifications from narrative fictions and put them to many uses—from vicarious sexual titillation to exploring taboo subjects with impunity. It is television that occupies us, as a rule, for something like 4 hours of our leisure time each day, and television brings us many narrative fictions every day, as Esslin (1982) points out.

The question that many media theorists and researchers are wrestling with now is, What effects are all these fictional narratives (which tend to be full of violence and sexuality) having on us? Art imitates life, according to Aristotle. (Of course, in the mass media, art imitates life in a highly distorted manner.) But is life now beginning to imitate art? With these distinctions between narrative fiction and everyday life in mind, let us consider a number of aspects of everyday life that have narrative elements in them—that is, that have linear, sequential dimensions to them and, generally speaking, some kind of resolution—dramatic or otherwise.

Jokes as Narratives

A joke may be defined as a short fictional narrative, meant to amuse others, that ends with a punch line. There are many ways of creating humor other than by telling jokes: A person can use insult, victim humor (insult directed at oneself), exaggeration, sarcasm, absurdity, allusion, facetiousness, and so on. I list and explain 45 basic techniques found in humor in my book *An Anatomy of Humor* (1993). These techniques are also, I should point out, often found in jokes.

What is distinctive about jokes is that they are narratives that are resolved by punch lines. Each element or part of a joke we can call a jokeme. When you have a string of jokemes that end in a punch line, which "creates the humor," you have a joke. Jokes take the following form:

$$A \rightarrow B \rightarrow C \rightarrow D \rightarrow E \rightarrow F \rightarrow G \rightarrow H \text{ (punch line)}$$
$$\uparrow$$
$$I \text{ (laughter)}$$

Here A through G represent the parts of the joke (that is, the jokemes) that lead up to H, the punch line, a surprise resolution of the narrative. The punch line gives the joke "meaning" and generates laughter.

As an illustration, let me offer one of my favorite jokes:

A   A man goes to Miami for vacation.

B   After three days in the sun, he notices that he has a glorious tan all over his body except for his penis.

C   The next day, he goes to a deserted part of the beach, takes off all his clothes, and puts sand all over himself until only his penis is sticking out in the sun.

D   A short while later, two little old ladies come walking by. One notices the penis and points it out to her friend.

E   "When I was 20, I was scared to death of them."

F   "When I was 40, I couldn't get enough of them."

G   "When I was 60, I couldn't get one to come near me."

H   *"And now they're growing wild on the beach!"*

I   (laughter)

This narrative, like many narratives, not only gives pleasure (by amusing us), it also reveals something about life—and, in this case, human sexuality and, in particular, feminine desire. We laugh at this joke because of the man's absurd behavior and because the woman has made a mistake (they're growing wild on the beach) that reflects her suppressed sexual desire (growing wild on the beach and therefore available to all).

One thing about jokes is that they are, generally speaking, performances of someone else's material. Most people don't, as a rule, create their own jokes. We may make spontaneous witty remarks or good puns from time to time, but we usually don't create original jokes. So telling a joke is a performance, on our part, of a text; usually these texts are anonymous. We don't know who made them up or where they come from, but we find them amusing and tell them for a number of reasons: to increase our popularity, to amuse, to entertain, to arouse others sexually, and so on.

There is usually a good deal of hostility and aggression in jokes, and when jokes "fall flat" it is usually because this aggression is too overt. Jokes reveal a great deal about the mind-sets and psychological hang-ups of the people in the societies in which they are told, and so are valuable texts for social scientists. Like all narratives, jokes can be used to control people and often have a coercive dimension to them.

But jokes also often counter the power structure and function as a means of resistance. Examples of this use of jokes include many of those

A joke is a play upon form. It brings into relation disparate elements in
such a way that one accepted pattern is challenged by the appearance
of another which in some way was hidden in the first. I confess that I
find Freud's definition of the joke highly satisfactory. The joke is an
image of the relaxation of conscious control in favour of the
subconscious. For the rest of this article I shall be assuming that any
recognizable joke falls into the joke pattern which needs two elements,
the juxtaposition of a control against that which is controlled, this
juxtaposition being such that the latter triumphs. Needless to say, a
successful subversion of one form by another completes or ends the
joke. It is implicit in the Freudian model that the unconscious does not
take over the control system. The wise sayings of lunatics, talking
animals, children and drunkards are funny because they are not in
control; otherwise they would not be an image of the subconscious.
The joke merely affords opportunity for realising that an accepted
pattern has no necessity. Its excitement lies in the suggestion that any
particular ordering of experience may be arbitrary and subjective. It is
frivolous in that it produces no real alternative, only an exhilarating
freedom from form in general.

Mary Douglas, *Implicit Meanings:*
Essays in Anthropology (1975, p. 96)

told in Eastern Europe about the Russians, socialism, the Communist
Party, the KGB, and related matters. Let me close this discussion of jokes
by offering some classic Russian jokes about Radio Erevan in Soviet
Armenia. These jokes take the following form: Someone asks Radio
Erevan a question, and it offers an answer.

A caller phones Radio Erevan and asks "Dear Radio Erevan—Would it
be possible to introduce socialism into the Sahara?"
"Yes," replies Radio Erevan. "But after the first Five-Year Plan, the
Sahara would have to import sand."

A caller phones Radio Erevan and asks, "Is it true that Comrade Kasparov
won 10,000 rubles at the lottery?"
"Yes, it is true," replies Radio Erevan. "But it wasn't Comrade
Kasparov but Comrade Smirnov, and it wasn't 10,000 rubles but 5,000
rubles, and he didn't win it at the lottery but lost it gambling.

Journals and Diaries

The differences between journals and diaries are difficult to specify, but for our purposes we will say a journal is essentially a workbook in which a writer sketches out ideas and comments on things, and a diary is a very personal record of an individual's activities and thoughts. This distinction will serve our purposes, even though some people's journals are like other people's diaries. Journals and diaries are generally written in books or notebooks, though many people keep them on computer disk nowadays.

Journals and diaries are texts that are written more or less on a day-to-day basis, and generally the entries are dated. Thus it is time that provides the organization for these texts, as the writers write about things that have happened to them, notions they have, dinners they've had, people they've met, their hopes, and so on. There is no plot to these texts, though after a number of years writers may be able to detect threads in them that they did not notice while writing them.

Unlike in the narratives found in the mass media, those who keep diaries and journals are the central characters, the heroes and heroines, of their texts. Individuals keep journals because the process of writing helps them to gain insights about themselves, clarifies ideas in their heads, and stimulates new ideas; further, journals provide records for their keepers to contemplate. Many find that keeping a journal has some therapeutic value; in a manner similar to that associated with Freud's "talking cure," journals offer those who keep them a "writing cure." Instead of talking to others, journal writers "talk to themselves," so to speak, carrying on dialogues (internal, but expressed in writing) that often reach into or shed light on preconscious and unconscious elements of their psyches.

Keeping a journal or diary is a literary act, and, like other creative efforts, it often taps into ideas and feelings the author has not even been aware of having. These texts are meta-autobiographies written in passing—unlike autobiographies written at given moments in time, usually when their authors are at a fairly advanced age, when they try to recapture the past. Autobiographers impose a thread of narrative to bind everything together. In diaries and journals, there is no thread that the author is aware of, other than the passing of time.

Conversations

Although we seldom give much thought to the matter, conversations are really a popular art form, and, as such, they have their own rules and conventions. George Lakoff and Mark Johnson discuss these conventions in their book *Metaphors We Live By* (1980). Discussing the most basic form of conversation, which involves two persons, they point out that a certain amount of cooperation is involved between the individual who initiates the conversation and the other person, who participates in taking turns and keeping the conversation on its topic or shifting to a different one.

> Even in as simple a case as a polite two-party conversation, several dimensions of structure can be seen:
>
> *Participants:* The participants are of a certain natural kind, namely, people. Here they take the role of speakers. The conversation is defined by what the participants do, and the same participants play a role throughout the conversation.
>
> *Parts:* The parts consist of a certain natural kind of activity, namely, talking. Each turn at talking is a part of the conversation as a whole, and these parts must be put together in a certain fashion for there to be a coherent conversation.
>
> *Stages:* Conversations typically have a set of initial conditions and pass through various stages, including at least a beginning, a central part, and an end. Thus there are certain things that are said in order to initiate a conversation ("Hello," "How are you?," etc.), others that move it along to the central part, and still others that end it.
>
> *Linear sequence:* The participants' turns at speaking are ordered in a linear sequence, with the general constraint that the speakers alternate. Certain overlappings are permitted, and there are lapses where one speaker doesn't take his turn and the other speaker continues. Without such constraints on linear sequencing of parts, you get a monologue or a jumble of words but no conversation.
>
> *Causation:* The finish of one turn at talking is expected to result in the beginning of the next turn.
>
> *Purpose:* Conversations may serve any number of purposes but all typical conversations share the purpose of maintaining polite social interaction in a reasonably cooperative manner. (pp. 77-78)

We can see, then, that conversations have a linear nature and thus function as narratives. If one of the persons involved in a conversation misses a cue, problems arise. Let me offer an example. At a dinner party I attended recently, the hostess asked one of the guests about a book the guest was writing. The conversation went something like this:

Hostess: I understand you're writing a book. Tell us something about it.
Guest: It's a textbook.
Hostess: End of conversation?

The hostess had asked a question to draw her guest out and enable the guest to tell the others present something about the book and get a new conversation going. When the guest said, "It's a textbook" and nothing else, the hostess, who wanted to provide an opportunity for her guest to talk, asked, very aptly, "End of conversation?" What she meant by this was that the guest had not seized the opportunity to continue the conversation. Once the hostess asked, "End of conversation?" the guest started discussing the book in more detail.

We see, then, that conversations take a certain amount of effort and involve creating fugitive narratives that are rule bound; to be able to converse, one must know the rules and follow them. People who do not follow the rules about turn taking and monopolize conversations are generally considered to be bores (and boors). As Ambrose Bierce puts it, a bore is "a person who talks when you wish him to listen." Now we turn to a special kind of conversation—psychotherapy.

Psychotherapy

People who undergo psychotherapy become involved in unique kinds of spoken dialogues with others—therapists who try to help them deal with problems they have (or, as those who are hostile to psychotherapy would put it, problems they think they have); Freud calls this the "talking cure." The therapeutic experience is, from a structural point of view, analogous to fictional narratives in that both have, or often have, tasks to be done, complications, flashbacks, crises, and leading figures or protagonists and antagonists (heroes and heroines, villains, and helpers for both).

The conversations that take place in the context of therapy are often like detective stories in that they deal with discovering or uncovering some "villain" and understanding that person's motivations and the motivations of the person undergoing therapy as well. Therapeutic work also often resembles spy stories in which one has to find the "mole," the member of the organization (or spy "family") who is sabotaging things, giving information to the enemy, and acting as a double agent. Some psychotherapy is endless, like a television serial (like a soap opera—and often in other respects also); in other cases, psychotherapy is bounded by an agreement between the parties to end the therapy after a certain number of sessions.

Therapy can be seen, then, as a kind of dramatic autobiographical narrative text in which the client plays the central role, a two-person play of sorts in which the client responds to questions and comments by the other actor (the therapist) and tries to find some way of resolving a problem or conflict that may be internal, external, or a combination of the two. The therapist has a dual role, as both player and audience, and it is what the therapist hears as the audience that shapes what he or she does as a player.

As in theatrical dramas, therapy often reaches a moment of crisis (in the Freudian view of things, that is), when a resolution to some problem suddenly appears, when there is at least the possibility of a satisfactory denouement. In some cases, that is enough to terminate the therapy; in others it is only one episode in a series of resolutions that need to be made.

Psychotherapy can be seen, then, as a kind of interactive play that clients "write" from week to week (or more often). What happens one week often affects what happens the next. The therapist also writes a kind of script, afterward, to indicate what has been done and how things are going.

Repeat Performances

We can also adopt a theatrical metaphor to look at most of our everyday experiences, what I call *repeat performances*. Every day, generally speaking, we do certain things: We get up and wash up, have breakfast, go off to work or school or wherever, work or study a while, have lunch, return to school or job, come home and have dinner, watch television or read a book or whatever, and go to bed.

Repeat performances may involve, at times, fighting for "love"; at other times, they may involve fighting for "glory" (or, often, just plain fighting). For the most part, however, they involve routines that don't vary much from day to day; most people seldom have to face a case of "do or die." Some of our repeat performances are repeated every day, others we do only on working days, and others are only periodic: going to religious services, shopping for groceries, going to the movies (or "going out," in a ritual manner, every Saturday night), and so on. Even vacations are periodic, though when we take vacations we try to get away from our routines by traveling to somewhere new or doing something "different."

We are all, in a sense, authors and playwrights, and our lives, the repeat performances, are the texts. These texts are not, as a rule, exciting, full of adventure and drama, but that does not make them any less important to us. We can introduce minor variations into our repeat performances—for instance, having bacon and eggs for breakfast one day, pancakes the next, and waffles the next—but the basic stuff of our lives is based on daily routines. There is a reason for this: Psychologically, we need stability and security; most of us cannot tolerate a life full of danger, threat, or wild excitement. (Continual danger and threat also can become routine, as a matter of fact. This explains why spies sometimes become careless and get caught.)

Our routines are, generally, the least problematic parts of our lives. The breaks from routine—accidents, sudden physical illnesses, the deaths of loved ones, getting fired—are the "bad news" parts of our lives. That is why "No news is good news" is often true.

If couples wish to marry and have families, they must provide homes and nurturing for their children, which means they must spend considerable amounts of time with the members of their families. It is very difficult to wander around the world, undertake heroic adventures, and have a stable family life at the same time.

As we age, our repeat performances change; the kinds of things we do, the parts we play in the dramas of our lives, vary. We may travel more, stay around the house and involve ourselves in hobbies more, or see doctors more routinely, for example. We move from playing the leads in our stories (the guy who gets the girl or vice versa) to supporting roles, so to speak. Katharine Hepburn has made an interesting comment about getting older that is relevant: "After seventy," she said, "every time you turn around, it's time for breakfast."

So, like the stars of long-running Broadway plays, who give the same performances (say the same lines over and over again) for months or years; our lives can be seen as repeat performances in which we are happy to be on the stage, to be able to repeat our performances, for as long as we can. Then, one day, the final curtain falls.

Obituaries

Obituaries are hyperreductionist microbiographies. They cover the high points of individuals' lives and, for most people, represent one of the few times their names are printed in a newspaper; the other times, if at all, are when they are born and when they get married. (Many people, of course, never have article-length obituaries in the papers; their names simply appear in listings of those who have died.) An obituary often has the tightness of drama, because it lists only the most important points of a person's life. An obituary reduces a life to a paragraph or two, in the ordinary case: the person's occupation, what family he or she leaves behind, any accomplishments, that kind of thing.

An obituary thus is a summary of a person's life and not a resolution of a story that puts everything into place and resolves various conflicts. This, of course, sometimes happens when a person dies, but it is always by chance. Obituaries are microbiographies, highly compressed texts. The size of an obituary and its location in a newspaper, as well as which newspapers it appears in, are signifiers of the deceased person's importance. The deaths of world-renowned personalities are often followed by the appearance of long articles about them, a functional alternative to the routinized obituary, on the first page of the *New York Times* and other important newspapers. Other newspapers often carry edited versions of obituaries of "important people" the next day.

There is one other point I want to make here. For important figures, or extremely notorious ones, obituaries are often written before their

deaths and are ready to be updated in a flash when the persons actually die. So one measure of what a person has achieved in life may be when the draft of his or her obituary is written. The more important one is, we could say, the earlier one's obituary is written.

The humorist Robert Benchley said that "the world is divided into two groups of people: those who divide the world into two groups of people and those who don't." In like manner, we can say that the world is divided into three groups of people: those who have their obituaries written before they die, those whose obituaries are written after they die, and those who die but don't have obituaries written about them at all.

A Note on Narratives and Everyday Life

I have dealt here with only a few of the areas in which we find narratives in our everyday lives; there are many others. An illness can be considered a narrative, for instance; it can actually take the form of a written narrative in the notes physicians make as an illness progresses. Confessions are also narratives: A criminal describes what he or she has done, usually in the form of a list of crimes.

Sporting events take narrative form also. They are often very exciting, because we don't know how they will be resolved (who will win). They have heroes or heroines, villains, crucial events, excitement, and risk. They are narratives that write their own scripts, so to speak, as they progress. (This is what we do with our lives, also.) And sometimes they are not resolved until the final seconds of the game, or in overtime.

Sports often provide people with vicarious excitement and a sense of triumph (or generate a sense of devastation from sudden defeat) that help give their lives increased color and affect. I often think that the less exciting or satisfying people's everyday lives are, the more they invest in the sports teams and sports figures with whom they identify.

There are thus many aspects of everyday life that have narrative dimensions to them, and social scientists are now beginning to recognize, and to study, the roles narratives play in people's lives and in society. We have to learn how to "read" narratives, to look at them analytically, to see analogies in them with aspects of our lives, to see what their heroes and heroines symbolize and the way these figures reflect as well as affect our ideas about power, sexuality, morality, the good life, and so on.

We used to think of the stories we read, listen to, and watch as little more than trivial amusements employed to "kill time." Now we know that people learn from stories, are emotionally affected by them, and actually need stories to lend color and interest to their everyday lives. That is why some scholars have described humans not as *Homo sapiens,* man and woman the knower, but as *Homo narrans,* man and woman the storytellers, the tellers of tales.

Appendix
Simulations, Activities,
Games, and Exercises

I have developed a number of simulations, activities, games, and exercises—which I refer to collectively as learning games—that involve applying various aspects of narrative theory to the popular arts and media. These learning games force players to move from the level of theory, where the concepts may be vague and their utility not terribly clear, to that of practice, where they can see how concepts and theories can help them to make sense of narratives as well as create them.

Generally speaking, when I have the students in my courses play such learning games, I divide the class into groups of three or four; all students in each group are required to participate in the activities, but I ask each group to select one member to function as the designated "scribe" (to do the actual writing). Many of these learning games also make suitable homework assignments, for individuals or for teams of players. However, it should be kept in mind that the emphasis in these learning games is on "play"; I've found that my students find them both enjoyable and valuable. In games that involve scripts, team members can take on roles to act out what is written. In other kinds of games, the "findings" of the various teams can serve as the basis of classroom discussion. Depending on the classroom, the class, and the context, variations on all of these learning games can be devised, of course, and new games can be created.

Anatomy of a Tale

In my discussion of Vladimir Propp's *Morphology of the Folktale* (1928/1968) in Chapter 2, I have shown how we can use Propp's functions to analyze a story. In this exercise, you are to write a story based on the set of Propp's functions listed below. To play this game, you should consult Table 2.1 and use the descriptions of the functions in writing your story. Remember that you can modernize things—thus, at the end, the hero need not literally marry a princess and ascend the throne.

Remember, when you write the story, to (a) use the past tense, (b) include description and dialogue, and (c) make sure there's action and conflict, to keep interest. (Do *not* write a fairy tale in this exercise.) Base your story on the following functions:

1. *Initial situation:* Members of family, hero introduced.
2. *Absentation:* One of the members of the family absents him- or herself.
3. *Interdiction:* Interdiction addressed to hero (can be reversed).
4. *Violation:* Interdiction is violated.
5. *Villainy:* Villain causes harm to member of the family.
6. *Mediation:* Misfortune made known, hero is dispatched.
7. *Receipt of agent:* Hero acquires use of magical agent.
8. *Spatial change:* Hero led to object of his search.
9. *Struggle:* Hero and villain join in combat.
10. *Branding:* Hero is branded.
11. *Victory:* Villain is defeated.
12. *Unfounded claims:* False hero is exposed.
13. *Wedding:* Hero is married, ascends the throne.

After the stories are written, teams or individuals should share their stories so that the larger group can see how different stories can be even when they use the same Proppian functions.

Paradigmatic Analysis

Lévi-Strauss (1967) has argued that the paradigmatic analysis of a text tells us what it "really" means, in contrast to a syntagmatic (Proppian) analysis of a text, which focuses on what happens. In this modification of Lévi-Strauss's methods, you will be looking at various paired oppositions that give a text meaning. Saussure (1966) has suggested that concepts are defined differentially; the same applies to characters in texts, their actions, and so on. Create a list of paired oppositions that can be elicited from the following quotation:

> In the beginning God created the heaven and the earth. And the earth was without form, and void; and darkness was upon the face of the deep. And the Spirit of God moved upon the face of the waters. And God said, "Let there be light": and there was light. And God saw the light, that it was good: and God divided the light from the darkness. And God called the light Day, and the darkness he called Night. And the evening and the morning were the first day.

Dream Analysis

According to psychoanalytic theory (and most psychologists would agree), dreams play a very significant role in our lives. Freud used his theories about symbolization, condensation, displacement, and so on, to analyze dreams. I've offered an example of Freud's analysis of a dream experienced by one of his patients in Chapter 5; now I offer a dream taken from Freud's (1900/1965) book on dreams and ask you to decode it, as best you can, using the concepts discussed in Chapter 5.

> I went into a kitchen in search of some pudding. Three women were standing in it; one of them was the hostess of the inn and was twisting something about in her hands, as though she was making Knodel [dump-

lings]. She answered that I must wait until she was ready. I felt impatient and went off with a sense of injury. I put on an overcoat. But the first I tried on was too long for me. I took it off, rather surprised to find it was trimmed with fur. A second one that I put on had a long strip with a Turkish design let into it. A stranger with a long face and a short pointed beard came up and tried to prevent my putting it on, saying it was his. I showed him then that it was embroidered all over with a Turkish pattern. He asked: "What have the Turkish (designs, stripes . . .) to do with you?" But we then became quite friendly with each other.

What sense can you make of the events that take place in this dream? In addition to analyzing this dream, you may wish to write down a dream you've had and try to analyze it.

Here is another dream to analyze, taken from a novel by D. M. Thomas, *The White Hotel* (1981). (In the novel the dream is recounted, and then a few pages later, a small portion of the dream that had been forgotten is recounted. I have inserted the forgotten fragment in boldface type here to differentiate it from the original recounting of the dream.) Try as best you can to make sense of the symbolic significance of the various events that happen in the dream.

I was travelling in a train, sitting across from a man who was reading. He involved me in conversation, and I felt he was being overfamiliar. **I said to the young man I was going to Moscow to visit the T—s, and he replied they wouldn't be able to put me up, and I'd have to sleep in the summer-house. It would be hot in there, he added, and I'd have to take my clothes off.** The train stopped in the middle of nowhere, and I decided to get out, to be rid of him. I was surprised that a lot of other people got out too, as it was only a small place and completely dead. But the platform signs said *Budapest,* which explained it. I pushed past the ticket collector, not wanting to show my ticket, because I was supposed to go on further. I crossed a bridge and found myself outside a house which had the number 29. I tried to open it with my key, but to my surprise it wouldn't open, so I went on past and came to number 34. Though my key wouldn't turn, the door opened. It was a small private hotel. There was a silver umbrella drying off in the hall, and I thought, My mother is staying here. I went into a white room. Eventually an elderly gentleman came in and said, "The house is empty." I was sorry for him because I knew what it contained. He said, in a dreadful voice, "My daughter is dead." He was so shocked and sorrowful I felt I didn't exist for him any more. (pp. 102-103, 107)

You might also want to record some of your own dreams, if you can remember them, and try to analyze them.

Writing a Therapeutic Fairy Tale

This exercise stems from the discussion in Chapter 6 of Bruno Bettelheim's *The Uses of Enchantment* (1976). Bettelheim recounts how traditional Hindu healers often compose individualized fairy tales for their patients to help them deal with their problems. The patients study the fairy tales and learn, by identifying with the characters, something about their problems and how to solve them.

In this exercise, pretend that you are a Hindu healer and are writing a fairy tale to help a person deal with an assortment of psychological afflictions. Please do the following:

▓ Write a traditional (not a modernized parody) fairy tale that starts "Once upon a time, long, long ago" and concludes "and so they all lived happily ever after." Use dialogue, description, and lots of action.

▓ Write in the past tense, and include typical characters from fairy tales: kings, queens, princes and princesses, dragons, animal helpers, heroes with names like "Jack" or "Tom."

▓ Have the actions of the characters reflect and provide resolutions for the numerous psychological problems of the person who has been assigned to you from the following choices:

  Person 1: Oedipus complex, castration anxiety, regression

  Person 2: penis envy, narcissism, rationalization

  Person 3: anal eroticism, ambivalence, fixation

  Person 4: Oedipus complex, narcissism, fixation

  Person 5: fixation, castration anxiety, narcissism

Origin Tales

Every comic book hero and heroine, or team of heroes and heroines, has an origin tale—a page or two in which the character is introduced to the audience. The most famous of these, no doubt, is the one for Superman, which tells of his origins on Krypton, his long travel in a spaceship to the planet Earth, his being found by the kindly couple who adopted him (the Kents), his great powers, and so on.

In this activity you are to draw an origin tale for a superhero or superheroine you have created. Draw your tale in 10 or 12 frames on a piece of paper or cardboard that is a standard size agreed to by all of the teams or individuals participating in this activity. Remember to observe the following rules:

- Use 10 or 12 frames. Make real drawings and color them in. Do not use stick figures.
- Have the characters speak in balloons. You can also use parts of panels to give continuity information.
- Pay attention to facial expressions, characters' clothing, action depictions, sound effects, and dialogue.
- Consider what special abilities, powers, and so on your hero or heroine has.
- Tell a story. Even though you are introducing your character to an audience, you still have to have action, conflict, and so on.

When completed, the origin tales of all participants should be exhibited together so that everyone can observe the different kinds of heroes, heroines, villains, monsters, and so on that have been created. Are there any similarities among the various figures or among the themes dealt with? What do the origin tales reflect about the age group of those creating the tales and about American culture and society?

Radio Scripts

Using the material in Table 10.1 as well as the example of a radio script in Chapter 10, write a radio script that parodies a well-known television program, such as *Star Trek, The Brady Bunch,* or *Northern Exposure.* Remember to follow these rules to create a script that appears in radio's traditional format:

- Divide the page into two columns. In the left-hand column, which should be about 1½ inches wide, use ALL CAPS for the names of the characters or indications for MUSIC or SFX (sound effects).

▦ Place instructions concerning music or sound effects, in ALL CAPS and underlined (or italicized), in the right-hand column.

▦ Use the right-hand column for the dialogue, always in caps and lower-case. (Having only the dialogue in caps and lowercase makes it easy to differentiate dialogue from other aspects of the script.)

▦ Place instructions about how a character is to read his or her lines or other action he or she is to take in ALL CAPS and in parentheses before or following the affected dialogue.

Following is an example in traditional radio script format:

SFX	*BAR SOUNDS: PEOPLE TALKING, LAUGHTER, ETC.*
JOHN	(ANGRILY) You stood me up last night. And this wasn't the first time.
GWEN	(COYLY) Please forgive me, John. I was so involved learning about narratives that I lost track of time.
MUSIC	*JUKEBOX PLAYS FRANK SINATRA SINGING "MY WAY"*
JOHN	I'm sorry, Gwen. But it's too late. We're finished.
GWEN	If that's the way you feel, it's fine with me. Besides, I was just in the middle of the chapter on dreams. Last night I dreamed you were a frog. What can that mean? (SHE TAKES BOOK OUT OF HER PURSE AND STARTS READING)

Television Narrative Analysis

In this exercise you will examine a television narrative in terms of some of the methods and concepts discussed in this book. After viewing the assigned narrative, do the following:

▦ Apply Propp's morphology to the text. Try to find six or eight of Propp's functions that are reflected in the television program. List all functions and describe the events in the text that exemplify each function.

▦ Make a paradigmatic analysis of the text; that is, list a series of paired oppositions that you find in the text. All the terms on the left side should relate to one another and be opposite to all the terms on the right side of your list.

▦ Try to decide which events in the text are the "kernels" and which are the "satellites."

▓ Think of the text as being a kind of "public" dream. Analyze the text in terms of the symbolic significance of the major events in the text. What might they reflect about politics, society, culture?

In group discussion after the above assignments have been completed, you should be able to justify your choices and be prepared to explain what you have done. If there are widespread disagreements about the application of these four ways of looking at the text, what does that mean?

Western Films

Watch *Shane* and analyze it by applying the various concepts discussed in Chapter 11 on film westerns. Some things to consider:

▓ How good is the acting?

▓ How significant is the casting? Is Alan Ladd believable in the title role? Is Jack Palance suited for his role? Justify your answers. Do you think it is the acting that "makes" the film, or something else? If so, what?

▓ How good is the writing in the script? Does the plot make sense?

▓ How would you apply Cawelti's (1971) notions about westerns to this film? Do you find his ideas useful? Do they provide you with any insights of importance?

▓ Will Wright (1975) sees *Shane* as a "classical" western—one in which a lone gunfighter saves a town or farmers. Do you agree? If that isn't the most important aspect of the film, what is?

▓ In *High Noon* a lone fighter saves the town. Why doesn't Wright consider *High Noon* a classical western? If you've seen both *High Noon* and *Shane*, which do you think is the better film? Which do you like better? Explain your answers.

▓ Westerns died out after the 1970s and haven't really staged a comeback. Why did they die out and why aren't people (in general) interested in westerns (or as interested as they used to be) anymore?

▓ Write a "short short" Western radio script in which you use as many of the conventions of the genre as you can.

Popular Fiction

In this activity, you are to take five novels from any one popular fiction genre—detective novels, spy novels, science fiction novels, or romances—and compare their first and last paragraphs. What does a comparison of these openings and closings reveal? Are there any similarities or differences of significance? What stylistic devices do you notice in these openings and endings? How much description do you find? How much dialogue? How much action? Does reading the openings make you want to continue with the books?

Here are some first paragraphs from some popular novels: Borden Chase's *Red River* (1948) (western), Ian Fleming's *Dr. No* (1958) (spy), Mary Shelley's *Frankenstein* (1818/1967) (horror), Arthur C. Clarke's *Rendezvous With Rama* (1974) (science fiction), and Agatha Christie's *Thirteen at Dinner* (1933/1969) (classical detective). Compare them and then discuss their literary style as well as the topics mentioned above.

Red River

His name was Thomas Dunson, born in Birkenhead across Mersey from Liverpool, come from England God knows how. A bull of a man. A brute of a man. Thick-necked, low-jowled, with eyes that looked out at you like the rounded gray ends of bullets in a pistol cylinder. And there he sat, all slumped like a bulging bag of grain on the wide seat of the Conestoga wagon. The hands that held the reins were heavy across the backs. The fingers were blunt, flat across the tips. His head rolled with the motion of the wagon as it lurched along over the flatlands.

Dr. No

Punctually at six o'clock the sun set with a last yellow flash behind the Blue Mountains, a wave of violet shadow poured down Richmond Road, and the crickets and tree frogs in the fine gardens began to zing and tinkle.

Frankenstein

Letter 1
    To Mrs. Saville, England
    St. Petersburgh, Dec. 11th, 17—
    You will rejoice to hear that no disaster has accompanied the commencement of the enterprise which you have regarded with such evil forebodings. I arrived here yesterday, and my first task is to assure my dear sister of my welfare and increasing confidence in the success of my undertaking.

Rendezvous With Rama

> Sooner or later it was bound to happen. On June 30, 1908, Moscow escaped destruction by three hours and four thousand kilometers—a margin invisibly small by the standards of the universe. On February 12, 1947, another Russian city had a still narrower escape, when the second great meteorite of the twentieth century detonated less than four hundred kilometers from Vladivostok, with an explosion rivaling that of the newly invented uranium bomb.

Thirteen at Dinner

> The memory of the public is short. Already the intense interest and excitement aroused by the murder of George Alfred St. Vincent Marsh, fourth Baron Edgware, is a thing past and forgotten. Newer sensations have taken place.

Quotations to Discuss

In this activity you will read and discuss the following quotations. What ideas and insights do they offer about narrative theory, authorial techniques, narratives in the popular arts and media, and related considerations? Are either of them dated? Do the authors make glittering generalizations, mistakes in fact, or any other kinds of errors? Look up any terms the authors use with which you are not familiar, so you can be very clear on what they are talking about.

> Soap operas present communities of as many as 40 characters, many of whom have been on the shows for years. The fans find most of the characters interesting; they identify with some, hate others, and love hating some. Importantly, they come to care what happens to the characters, and they see and interpret the story through characters' perspectives. . . . To interpret character psyches and see things from their perspectives, participants must draw on their own interpersonal and emotional experiences as well as other areas of expertise. Because soap characters live in a world where life is focused always on the personal, the familial, the relational, and above all, the emotional, viewers must bring their own knowledge of these realms to bear on interpretation. The viewers' relationship with characters, the viewers' understanding of socioemotional experience, and soap opera's narrative structure, in

which moments of maximal suspense are always followed by temporal gaps, work together to ensure that fans will use the gaps during and between shows to discuss with one another possible outcomes and possible interpretations of what has been seen. (Baym, 1995, p. 143)

The typical science fiction film has a form as predictable as a Western, and is made up of elements which, to a practiced eye, are as classic as the saloon brawl, the blonde schoolteacher from the East, and the gun duel on the deserted main street.

One model scenario proceeds through five phases:

(1) The arrival of the thing. (Emergence of the monsters, landing of the alien spaceship, etc.) This is usually witnessed or suspected by just one person, a young scientist on a field trip. Nobody, neither his neighbors nor his colleagues will believe him for some time. . . .

(2) Confirmation of the hero's report by a host of witnesses to a great act of destruction. . . .

(3) In the capital of the country, conferences between scientists and the military take place with the hero lecturing before a chart, map, or blackboard. A national emergency is declared. . . .

(4) Further atrocities. At some point, the hero's girlfriend is in grave danger. Massive counterattacks by international forces, with brilliant displays of rocketry, rays, and other advanced weapons, are all unsuccessful. Enormous military casualties, usually by incineration.

(5) More conferences, whose motif is: "They must be vulnerable to something." Throughout the hero has been working in his lab to this end. . . . Final repulse of the monster or invaders. Mutual congratulations, while the hero and his girlfriend embrace cheek to cheek and scan the skies sturdily. "But have we seen the last of them?" (Sontag, 1970, pp. 212-213)

References

Abrams, M. H. (1958). *The mirror and the lamp: Romantic theory and the critical tradition.* New York: W. W. Norton

Abrams, M. H. (1988). *A glossary of literary terms* (5th ed.). New York: Harcourt Brace.

Bal, M. (1985). *Narratology: Introduction to the theory of narrative* (C. van Boheemen, Trans.). Toronto: University of Toronto Press.

Barnet, S., Berman, M., & Burto, W. (1960). *A dictionary of literary terms.* Boston: Little, Brown.

Barthes, R. (1977). *Image-music-text* (S. Heath, Trans.). New York: Hill & Wang.

Barthes, R. (1988). *The semiotic challenge* (R. Howard, Trans.). New York: Hill & Wang.

Baym, N. K. (1995). The emergence of community in computer-mediated communication. In S. G. Jones (Ed.), *CyberSociety: Computer-mediated communication and community.* Thousand Oaks, CA: Sage.

Bellah, R. N., Madsen, R., Sullivan, W., Swidler, A., & Tipton, S. M. (1985). *Habits of the heart: Individualism and commitment in American life.* Berkeley: University of California Press.

Berger, A. A. (1991). *Media analysis techniques* (rev. ed.). Newbury Park, CA: Sage.

Berger, A. A. (1992). *Popular culture genres: Theories and texts.* Newbury Park, CA: Sage.

Berger, A. A. (1993). *An anatomy of humor.* New Brunswick, NJ: Transaction.

Berger, A. A. (1994). *Li'l Abner: A study in American satire.* Jackson: University Press of Mississippi.

Berger, A. A. (1995a). *Cultural criticism: A primer of key concepts.* Thousand Oaks, CA: Sage.

Berger, A. A. (1995b). *Essentials of mass communication theory.* Thousand Oaks, CA: Sage.

Bettelheim, B. (1976). *The uses of enchantment: The meaning and importance of fairy tales.* New York: Knopf.

Boggs, J. M. (1978). *The art of watching films: A guide to film analysis.* Menlo Park, CA: Benjamin/Cummings.

Bondebjerg, I. (n.d.). Popular fiction, narrative and the melodramatic epic of American television. In M. Skovmand (Ed.), *Media fictions*. Aarhus, Denmark: Aarhus University Press.

Brenner, C. (1974). *An elementary textbook of psychoanalysis*. Garden City, NY: Anchor.

Brooks, P. (1984). *Reading for the plot: Design and intention in narrative*. New York: Knopf.

Bruner, J. (1986). *Actual minds, possible worlds*. Cambridge, MA: Harvard University Press.

Cantril, H. (1966). *The invasion from Mars: A study in the psychology of panic*. New York: Harper Torchbooks.

Carroll, L. (1960). *Alice's adventures in Wonderland & Through the looking glass*. New York: Signet Classics. (Original works published 1865 and 1872)

Cawelti, J. (1971). *The six-gun mystique*. Bowling Green, OH: Bowling Green University Popular Press.

Chase, B. (1948). *Red River*. New York: Bantam.

Chatman, S. (1978). *Story and discourse: Narrative structure in fiction and film*. Ithaca, NY: Cornell University Press.

Christie, A. (1940). *Murder on the Orient Express*. New York: Pocket Books.

Christie, A. (1969). *Thirteen at dinner*. New York: Dell. (Original work published 1933)

Clarke, A. C. (1974). *Rendezvous with Rama*. New York: Ballantine.

Culler, J. (1975). *Structuralist poetics: Structuralism, linguistics, and the study of literature*. Ithaca, NY: Cornell University Press.

de Certeau, M. (1984). *The practice of everyday life* (S. Rendall, Trans.). Berkeley: University of California Press.

Douglas, M. (1975). *Implicit meanings: Essays in anthropology*. London: Routledge & Kegan Paul.

Eisenstein, S. (1975). *The film sense*. Bloomington: Indiana University Press.

Esslin, M. (1982). *The age of television*. San Francisco: W. H. Freeman.

Fleming, I. (1958). *Dr. No*. New York: Signet.

Freud, S. (1963). The occurrence in dreams of material from fairy tales. In P. Rieff (Ed.), *Sigmund Freud: Character and culture*. New York: Collier.

Freud, S. (1965). *The interpretation of dreams* (J. Strachey, Trans.). New York: Avon. (Original work published 1900)

Fromm, E. (1957). *The forgotten language: An introduction to the understanding of dreams, fairy tales and myths*. New York: Grove.

Hammett, D. (1972). *The Maltese Falcon*. New York: Vintage. (Original work published 1930)

Hinsie, L. E., & Campbell, R. J. (1970). *Psychiatric dictionary* (4th ed.). New York: Oxford University Press.

Holquist, M. (1981). Preface. In M. M. Bakhtin, *The dialogic imagination: Four essays* (M. Holquist, Ed.; M. Holquist & C. Emerson, Trans.). Austin: University of Texas Press.

Inge, M. T. (1990). *Comics as culture*. Jackson: University Press of Mississippi.

Iser, W. (1988). The reading process: A phenomenological approach. In D. Lodge (Ed.), *Modern criticism and theory: A reader*. White Plains, NY: Longman. (Original work published 1972)

Jakobson, R. (1985). *Verbal art, verbal sign, verbal time* (K. Pomorska & S. Rudy, Eds.). Minneapolis: University of Minnesota Press.

James, H. (1934). *The art of the novel: Critical prefaces*. New York: Charles Scribner's Sons.

Jameson, F. (1972). *The prison-house of language: A critical account of structuralism and Russian formalism*. Princeton, NJ: Princeton University Press.

Kitses, J. (1969). *Horizons west*. Bloomington: Indiana University Press.

Kolbenschlag, M. (1981). *Kiss Sleeping Beauty good-bye: Breaking the spell of feminine myths and models.* New York: Bantam.

Kurtz, B. (1977). *Spots: The popular art of American television commercials.* New York: Arts Communications.

Lakoff, G., & Johnson, M. (1980). *Metaphors we live by.* Chicago: University of Chicago Press.

Lévi-Strauss, C. (1967). *Structural anthropology.* Garden City, NY: Doubleday.

Lotman, J. M. (1977). *The structure of the artistic text* (G. Lenhoff & R. Vroon, Trans.). Ann Arbor: Michigan Slavic Contributions.

Luthi, M. (1984). *The fairytale as art form and portrait of man* (J. Erickson, Trans.). Bloomington: Indiana University Press.

Lyotard, J.-F. (1984). *The postmodern condition: A report on knowledge.* Minneapolis: University of Minnesota Press.

McCloskey, D. N. (1990). Storytelling in economics. In C. Nash (Ed.), *Narrative in culture.* London: Routledge.

McLuhan, M. (1965). *Understanding media: The extensions of man.* New York: McGraw-Hill.

Morson, G. S. (1984). The war of the Well(e)s. In M. J. Medhurst & T. W. Benson (Eds.), *Rhetorical dimensions in media: A critical casebook.* Dubuque, IA: Kendall-Hunt.

Propp, V. (1968). *Morphology of the folktale* (2nd ed.) (L. Scott, Trans.). Austin: University of Texas Press. (Original work published 1928)

Queneau, R. (1981). *Exercises in style* (B. Wright, Trans.). New York: New Directions.

Richardson, L. (1990). Narrative and sociology. *Journal of Contemporary Ethnography, 19,* 116-135.

Riessman, C. K. (1993). *Narrative analysis.* Newbury Park, CA: Sage.

Saussure, F. de. (1966). *A course in general linguistics* (W. Baskin, Trans.). New York: McGraw-Hill.

Schnitzler, A. (1897/1955). La Ronde: Ten dialogues. In E. Bentley (Ed.), *Modern theatre* (Vol. 2). Garden City, NY: Anchor.

Scholes, R. (1974). *Structuralism in literature.* New Haven, CT: Yale University Press.

Shelley, M. (1967). *Frankenstein.* New York: Bantam. (Original work published 1818)

Shklovsky, V. (1989). Art as technique. In R. C. Davis & R. Schleifer (Eds.), *Contemporary literary criticism: Literary and cultural studies* (2nd ed.). New York: Longman.

Smith, J. H., & Parks, E. W. (1951). (Eds.). *The great critics: An anthology of literary criticism* (3rd ed.; S. H. Bucher, Trans.). New York: W. W. Norton.

Sontag, S. (1970). The imagination of disaster. In *Against interpretation:* New York: Dell.

Spiegelman, A. (1986). *Maus: A survivor's tale.* New York: Pantheon.

Spillane, M. (1947). *I, the Jury.* New York: Signet.

Thomas, D. M. (1981). *The white hotel.* New York: Viking.

Thrall, W. F., Hibbard, A., & Holman, C. H. (1960). *A handbook to literature* (rev. ed.). New York: Odyssey.

Todorov, T. (1981). *Introduction to poetics* (R. Howard, Trans.). Minneapolis: University of Minnesota Press.

Wells, H. G. (1964). *The war of the worlds.* New York: Airmont. (Original work published 1898)

Wright, W. (1975). *Sixguns and society: A structural study of the western.* Berkeley: University of California Press.

Name Index

Subject Index

About the Author

Arthur Asa Berger is Professor of Broadcast and Electronic Communication Arts at San Francisco State University, where he has taught since 1965. He has written extensively on media, popular culture, and related concerns. Among his recent books are *Cultural Criticism: A Primer of Key Concepts* (1995), *Essentials of Mass Communication Theory* (1995), *Manufacturing Desire: Media, Popular Culture, and Everyday Life* (1996), and *The Genius of the Jewish Joke* (1997). This volume is his twenty-seventh book and his eighth book for Sage Publications.

Dr. Berger had a Fulbright scholarship to Italy in 1963 and taught at the University of Milan. He has lectured extensively on media, popular culture, and related subjects in more than a dozen countries, including Brazil, Thailand, Italy, Germany, the Scandinavian countries, China, Taiwan, and Turkey. He is film and television review editor for *Society* magazine, editor of a series of reprints titled *Classics in Communication and Mass Culture,* and a consulting editor for *Humor* magazine. He has appeared on *20/20* and *The Today Show,* and he appears frequently on radio and television in the San Francisco Bay Area.

He is married to Phyllis Wolfson Berger, who teaches philosophy at Diablo Valley College, and has a son who is a mathematician and a daughter who is a screenwriter. His hobbies include theater, hiking, dining in ethnic restaurants, and traveling. He is also a cartoonist, and he drew cartoons for the *Journal of Communication* for more than a dozen years. He has illustrated a number of his own books and books by other authors.